ADMONISHED
A DOCTRINE OF DEFIANCE

Chronicle 28
B3STOW™

Panagiota Makaronis

KREA PREA™ Est. 2012

ISBN: 978-1-7644581-0-8

Cover design; Co Pilot
B3STOW™
Edited; KREA PREA™ Est. 2012
Written in: Australia Melbourne Victoria Craigieburn

I dedicate B3STOW™ Admonished; A Doctrine of Defiance Chronicle 28, to those who took me in & thought using me; will get them in. I have no idea who you are or what you want! I cannot help thinking your method was to outdo me.

It is outdated; It has been done & documented.

You lured your way into my existence like predator. On the purpose of harming me. That method you used to get in without my knowledge had me in Hiatus. I could not understand why I felt not grounded, uneasy overwhelmed & overzealous.

You had me locked in cornered so you can win. All because you knew how passionate I was; for you knew I would not give into you otherwise. I had no time to praise you, nor play your dirty games, or dirty tricks; from your dirty little secret.

The game you played was a gamble from an Assumption; it made you wiser than the rest you think! You were a Pest the way you entered was absolutely fragmented. You were not welcome I do not remember letting you in nor giving you an opportunity to use me to get in.

I am not Free; you were feeding off me & my spirit so you can get in & win. What I had to go through, to get out of that mess to see who you were had me hit a hold up.

I hit back towards your end three-fold!

I survived it; I will make sure you never do.

The saying never, say never does not apply to this vendetta.

Reap what you Sow!

Now that you are here & we have connected! Do me a Favour Bestow me & disconnect; if I played a role in your journey on the purpose for you to grow & harm me along the way, while you charm others to press replay;

What can I say: Pay me what you owe me with interest! This is a debt not a threat!

In the meantime; I curse you too & I hope you never get there & if you do & you need me or whomever to repeat. Do not return nor delay or press replay;

Just press Delete, Delete, Delete!

Profanities all the way!

Reset All

Have a nice day!

The challenges we seek are farfetched.
There is no vision in the mission.
Just a competition to preach your truth & prey on those who endeavour; to put you in a vendetta.

PANAGIOTA MAKARONIS

CONTENTS

By Panagiota Makaronis B3STOW™ • KREA PREA™

Est. 2012

Where theatrical disgrace meets ritual indictment.

Invocation beneath the Beast.

He who created that piece, had fast forwarded & hit me a feast.
Time to release that beast, that warned me.
I hit the end of that Feat.
With a curse I cannot not rehearse, because I come first & last.
Ever so; fasting for a feast
so I can release Peace & diminish that Beast!

With mind, Body & Spirit! Amen.

INTRODUCTION

Chronicle 28 Admonished A Doctrine of Defiance B3STOW™; The adventures continue, my journey up to now was a fight; with who? Only the corrupt knew. An assumption from within, made me see clearly, I was not wrong; my intuition did not serve me wrong. I felt my privacy was being invaded.

The rumours continued, those who were in on it were supposedly; knights in shining armour. The torment, the derogatory remarks continued it made me sense someone else was up to no good. Wanting to catch up, by sabotaging my existence. I became entertained; by the whole concept.

I felt overwhelmed, tormented without an explanation. The shocks to my system had me releasing endorphins; a competition was coming to fruition. It was encouraging the corrupt to keep feeding off me. It had me facing an anxiety I could not fight off; that is when I knew my psyche, was being attack.

An individual who had entered my realm, unwelcome; had attached to my etheric cord. How he got in; God knows. I must have made a mistake, and without my knowledge; let him in. The freedom of competing with me was apparently in sight; eyes on the prize, where we were neck and neck.

I was out numbered he had more man power that I; it threw me off track. Where my spirit had no choice but to intervene. Where I ended up was not clean; it was dirty, no clarity inbetween. One leg to stand on, my wing wounded and I injured. I had to heal, repeat, elevate get back on track and designate.

By now, the pain took over the game, and I on the mend healing; a wound that was oozing. All I knew I had to cut him off and feed off the clue; creating little pieces of terror. Just to harm he who harmed me like no other. To top it off, he had others working in unison to claim his truth.

The game was overdone; blaming me for every damn outcome. Not only they made me out to be a fabricator, I whinging; while they were succeeding. Eventually, thanks to who; It went viral the plan backfired and I fell out of that trap. An exit out of that damn deception; from that redemption.

Waiting for the corrupt to return so I can break the chain; caused an effect. I was to feed off it, this time around; I win every sound, thump, and trace; that put them in my vicinity, in the first place. The mission ended, it took that vision to a new level. My submissive approach, took over the submission.

I gave in on the condition; I catch the culprit from within. It was my way of accepting truth and creating an energy that had me face the end of that trace. It caused an effect took me on a journey that had me resurrect. I had to return a civility to that favour; that handed me a fear like no other.

The drama I had to endure, had me facing passive aggressive approach. Towards a journey that was, down to earth. I on a path with no freedom to release the demon; just wisdom. I was trying to get out of a dilemma. A delayed response to an ordeal, it had me feed off the trace; ignoring the truth.

For that reason, the trial became trivial, and an error where they journey became a terrible act of kindness. It had me feeding off the trace, lining me up for one more reason and that was to spoil the corrupts mission. If I was to speak out sooner than later; that would be worse than initial terror.

The ulterior motive, created an inertia, and an empty promise; no empathy what so ever. I was left forced to hit back in the long run naturally. When? I had no idea, for all I knew I was locked in a conspiracy that was to jeopardise my future endeavours. Handing the corrupt a chance to return.

It hit me with a vendetta; a task I knew nothing of; until I was hit by a profit. It was all done behind closed doors, assuming because I was not directly in on it; there would be no trace no case no final. Just an interrogation to the next destination. For I could sense trouble ahead; an energy taking over.

A hit run, on that double agent an end of a passageway; a reminder, of a past influence. It had me facing decades of dead ends, a façade; causing effects. It had me release, relapse, and refresh; while I get back on track and start fresh. The trace to that case was an invention, that needed attention.

I was seen as an easy, target; forcing their way in,

then return create intervention at the end of that manifestation. I had to trace that case, cause an effect terrorise that informal investigation that turned into an interrogation. In addition, conclude a follow up on a conspiracy theory.

I had no freedom to acclaim another intrusion because the game was intrinsic. What had given me a chance to return, had hit back with a flood of information in advance; that served me well. Based on a past event where I had to release that beast and uncover up another feast.

I was forcing myself to renew an overview; stepping into an overdrive. The curse had been rehearsed by those who were rejuvenated by my spirit. I was to reverse, condition the mission all so I can come first. The goal was set in stone, by he who led the pact; creating a delay to that redemption.

For who knew, had hired those who had a clue. They entered my realm and forced their way in returning the favour; handing me another warning. I was taken in, left to face another inning, towards a direction that will harm those who entered my realm; unwelcome.

I was on edge, trapped in the middle of an upcoming riddle. Hitting an energy that took me in and forced me to repeat a rebate from within. I had to fight back case close and create a trace that had me forced to hit back with remorse. A prewritten task by he who had an ego; tried to screw me.

It was traumatic, I had no idea what was going on and how deep I was is in it. The intent to purposely drive me towards another realm of insanity beyond rationality became the corrupts way of breaking the silence and feeding the redemption that handed me a misconduct of failed communication.

For he who had it in for me, wanted to see me fail. It brought my confidence level towards an entourage. An incur came to my attention, restoring my energy relighting my spirit and sparking up an event taking my truth towards another level. It took me on a journey that had me face reality.

It had me replacing that energy that forced me to interrogate, those who used me to get in. It had me feed off the trace from within. Just to find peace, from a vicious lie that was so brutal. It gave me a chance to hit back at the end of that trend; brought forward; leading me towards a presentation.

A lead, with reservation, and motivation for success. A journey where I get in and accompany the corrupt towards a passageway where they get in and lose everything. Handing them the loss to that freedom that created fear. A forced event to return break that cycle; haunting me at every recital.

It formed a trace that served me well at the end of that spell. It presented them with a challenge I was left to enter. A realm where every trace became a force to be reckoned with. Where this time around the corrupt were on the edge, trapped in the middle of a pledge; nowhere to turn.

The turn of events had changed; it gave me a chance to follow up on another train of thought. It presented me with a key that handed me the energy to release that beast. It forced me off the edge straight into a new improved journey. A trend that was on trapping those who had to reconsider.

They were way to busy trying to follow up on a brand-new key. An opportunity to break the chain, came too no cycle to attach to. It was left to chance a memory; part of a quick glance. When I hit the truth, the drama caved. The corrupt had nowhere to turn; but back to me, the enemy.

An energy that had me forced it caused an effect. It gave me a second chance to hit back with remorse. For the trace was based on a case, to test the patience of those who a cut off, those who knew. For those who had a clue had turned against he who knew; a gamble that fell into an uproar.

My conclusion was those who knew, tricked those who had a clue. Creating a war in peace so they can get through. What I assumed; I never truly knew. But those individuals hiding behind the scenes were wearing masks. It separated us from a journey; a chance to give in and undo that tradition.

It had me break the silence, the system; with a divine calling. A critical analysis had me wonder; did I truly know, or had I been taught a lesson by the Universe. A discrete who saw me easy failed. Even though the target was aimed towards me, all it did was turn back time. Creating a brand-new chime.

CHAPTER 1

◆ ◆ ◆

PRETEND IT'S THE END; IT'S JUST THE BEGINNING

I was handed freedom, and my talent was conditioned by the corrupts final mission. Apparently, I was in it, purely to give those who conspired to get me down; a chance to win it. It was harming me from within. I was stuck in a time warp, waiting for the trace to serve me well.

It presented me with a forthcoming spell. A challenge that had me face the end of that trend. It was warning me I hit a dead end. Creating a force that will hand me remorse an added task that will serve me well at the end of that spell. I was to cave in on the win, trace that trap.

It was part of a given to hand the corrupt a chance to confess. It had me on the edge, ready and willing to compete, compel and force the corrupt to go through hell. All while entering that trend that will hand me the key to victory. Then when the time come face another outcome.

It gave me the energy to get back on track, face my fear from within. Then when the time come repeat and start again. This time around I am no longer pretending, nor am I returning to repeat another yearning. For my intentions are real my foundation is ready to release that beast.

For the end result had come and gone, I was to overcome and face another outcome. It had me failing every game challenge a return, reap a reward and face another encore. For the outcome was surreal, it had me facing another reel. For trace at the end of the race was invalid.

It gave me the reward, that had me face another encore. It served me well. It gave me the thrill and the energy to recall another trace to that case. It had me face another fear. It forced me to release that beast that gave me a second chance to hit back in advance.

A time out had come and gone; it forced me to repeat and follow up on another trace. It had me on the edge ready to pledge, waiting patiently to validate and escape another trend. It formed an alliance that had me face another trace. It gave me a second trial to hit the corrupt back with denial.

It had me forced to hit back with remorse. Where I am given the impression that every trace had me face another warning. It hit with a challenge that took me in and faced me with a trend at the end. Where a hint of madness case closed handing me an invasion to that condition.

It forced me to hit back with repetition, where I was given the interpretation to hit a treason. For the edge of reason had me followed up on a tradition that favoured the corrupt at every mission. For I hit a challenge that served me well it gave me the energy to face another synergy.

Every fear factor, served a purpose and an invasion to that investigation. It took me on a pathway, leading me astray. I had no foundation to remain vigilant; every time I tried to make a mark I would hit a downside. The corrupt were on the other end waiting for me to fall, for another lie again.

Because I gave in, I had no choice but to reclaim my truth and rejoice. I was cornered by the corrupts trace. It had me facing another trend, it led me to a presentation that had me wait for the curse to reverse. So, when the time come, I could regain consciousness and start again.

It had me repeating a meeting, restoring my energy facing another siren that took me in and fed off me from within. It forced me to report, take a moment, and hit back with a curse I can rehearse. For those who hit me back and faced me with a test; had served me well at the end of that request.

Then wait patiently for me to fail, all so they hey can return and pretend. Leaving me waiting for the calm to end. All while I continue to release the beast; face a new feast. Trace a condition to that admiration that handed me another investigation, just to treat me as an outcast to their free ride.

It had me state a fact, stand on trial all while I feed of the edge of that final pledge. It had me face another trend then when the time come pretend. All while I prepare myself for a dead end. Claim my vision hit back with a proposition while the mission had me facing another competition.

It had me feeding off the redemption, that handed me deception. It created an expense to that will, handing me the hope to repeat and remain silent. All so I catch up and face another unethical invasive approach to that trace; that had me face another case.

All while I trace, hit back with the same old game. Fighting back those who hit me; ran on a conclusion. An achievement that had me on trial. So, when I reached my pinnacle, I could redo embrace feed off the condition and prepare myself for another competition to that mission.

I was on the run, waiting for the corrupt to hit me in the long run. There was no way I was going to let my guard down and allow them to return for another yearning. Then on a given moment a chance to hit back in advance. Waiting for the corrupt to return for another turn.

I tried to remain the same, assuming the trial and the error will not get me down. But it ran its cause and I again stuck in a rut fighting a lost cause. I had to enter rise above and beyond the hype I need to portray and pretend that every trace will praise me no longer, handing me a dead end.

I had to release that demon in the end, fight back and start again. For he whom was harming me was starving me he gave me an entrance to that mission that forced me off the edge straight into another competition. I was working freely under the raider and he on the hand was planning a hit.

Unfortunately, the trace had become unbearable. I had to face an entrance that was terribly wrong. It had me follow through, a trip down memory lane. A trace that forced me to embrace that energy that took me in. I hit a down fall and the trend had me facing a dead end in the end.

It was entertaining, me, with the notion the corrupt were returning for a repetition. It had me entering common ground, relying on the corrupt at every final trace. Leading me to a destination that had me refined. It caused an effect broke the silence repeated each stepping stone.

Because I had already lived it, I found myself reliving a dramatic effect. The drama had become a repeat and I was reliving a debt. I was given the opportunity to rise above and beyond, forced to restore my energy all so I can release that beast. It was haunting me at the end of that feast.

For what I thought was a given, handed me a trace at the end of that mission. I was left to repeat rebel and follow up on another spell. Just to give the corrupt a chance to own up, handing me the key I needed to break the cycle and rebuild with a defect on the other side.

A decision to that addition became an addiction because my prediction was followed up by a proposition. It handed me an evaluation that paused an effect and presented with a final defect. It was to bring forth redemption follow up on a release. Then when the time come face another fact.

A proposal that will lead me to a place that will have me accomplish a goal. A trace that will bring me forward, challenging me at the end of that trend. I was given a trap that had me relapse towards a tradition that had me repeating the wrong. Giving recognition to those who have no vision.

I had to follow up on a prediction; it had me revise another competition to that mission. For the advice given was part of a vision that was given to me by he who was not accomplishing anything. He needed to disclaim my honour, face me with a dishonour; feed of the trace gambling every case.

So, when I reached that peak, I could take it all in and face another win. Where the only thing left was to repeat, restore release that beast that had me face another feast. It had me rise above and beyond. I was led to believe that the test was purely to suppress my anxieties and move on.

Face another competition and override a failed proposition. It had me facing another competition, one heart felt curse after the next. It had me reverse take back my power and belt the corrupt every time I divide conquer, devour that trace and belted me at the end of the race.

While they rest rehearsed, and fed from within. A decision was made that had me sit in admin. It was part of a compelling event, that gave me the proposition to vent. I was taught a lesson left to repeat, just to give the corrupt a chance to delete and delay that game; gambling my life away.

A challenge that brought me forth, help me resurrect from that defect. It had me face another trace, a given opportunity to erase that challenge, so when I hit the end of that trend the only thing left to do was reveal and review another clue. Trapped in the middle of that final fluke.

It was based on a feast that had me release. It was part of a trend that gave me permission to pretend. A destination that took me on a long path. A trace that had me trapped; lining me up for a feast. It served me well at the end of that spell. Blinded by a contract, that was denied in the end.

It took me on a journey where I binged. Bathed in the corrupts filth, a lead handing them a trend. It served me well at the end of that trial. I was forced to repeat and regain conscious awareness again. without having to put up with the same game. For those who hit me ran hit with a huge impact.

It forced me off the edge, facing me with a curse; it put me on a path that had me lose faith. I was less likely to eradicate. Because each trace took a gamble, and left me hitting an entrance that led me towards a pathway of returning for another deception to that redemption.

A hint had me sitting on a royal Fush; my Dynasty was about to erupt. An energy that faced me, haunted me right through. It was leading me to a destination, that served me a final test an exploitation. I gave in, faced a tradition while on the move, taught a lesson delaying the inevitable.

An expectation that took me on a path, of emotional blackmail. A damnation hit me with redemption from that deception it became my manifestation. It took me on a journey that had me face another conservation. A momentum to hit back and finalise the impact.

Where I fell and I had to get back up and the only way I could was play with the corrupt. For the anecdote went way to far, it turned against me and left me facing a failed reality. It was leading me towards a wrong move. A reality to that trial that error and that had hit me with a final vendetta.

A challenge that forced me to hit back, it caused an effect and handed me a way out. Hinting to others; to follow the same route. Where I stood my ground, enough to realize the journey I was on, was a lie. It had me facing another trace, to that case that caused an effect.

It handed me the entrance to a pathway that forced me off the edge. It formed an alliance that had me hit back on the rebound. I was on the edge stirring, those who were stirring the pot. It gave me a second chance to hit back; with a brand-new plot. I was taught a lesson left to return the favour.

It had me face another trace on the edge, releasing that demon that had me rise above and beyond that confusion. Delaying what was to come from that outcome, I could not resist nor release. It forced me to hit back from that feast so I can find peace. Added with a confession at that deception.

It was part of a trend, that handed me a key to redeem a theme in the end. It gave me a chance to hit back in advance. Because I was taught a lesson it left me to release the beast to improve my circumstances and prove I was innocent. It took me back in time torn in more than direction.

I had to face a fear that led me to disappear. returning now, will bring the corrupt back down to earth. No more taking the piss out of that trend. Provoking me through ridicule bring forth gratitude to those who saw me as an easy target. It was yanking my chain, terrorising the corrupts method.

Time to break the system, tear it apart and have me face a dead end. It forced me to release that everlasting feast.

It pushed me in the corner and held me acclaim; just to find peace at the end of the game. I was off trying to make a mark, facing another trace at the end of the race.

It had me on the move, fast forward restoring my energy. It had me trapping those who disturb my peace. I was way off trying to catch up, state a fact create an impact. Where that lie that had me face another trace to get by. Had me back on track hitting back with an impact.

It created a task to break the silenced cycle. It forced me to hit back with a decipher. Because I was hit with a trace, that had me return for an entrapment. The case forced me to hit back a trace that had me face a curse; just to help the corrupt come first. It was part of a loyal discerning effect.

It had me reach that preach that forced me to press delete. It delayed a troubled trend along the way. A disadvantage to that tremor took its toll. It restored my energy and face me with a tremor a follow up to that dilemma. For I was left to pretend portray and start again.

CHAPTER 2

◆ ◆ ◆

FACE ME NOW CORRUPT! CAN YOU?

From the beginning I had to many bystanders who wanted to challenge me. They took me in and faced me with a trace that forced me to repeat. I had to redo, and accomplish a clue. One that was lingering in the back of my mind, where I did not want to waste time; looking for answers.

I Reached my pinnacle with a dead end; repairing it. Repeat a trial that had me living in denial. Where the energy that created the piece had me appear; encouraging me to erase. Cut the cord, break the chain, create a tremor, delete, and delay. Feeding off the corrupts method all the way.

It had me forced to hit back with remorse; undo that clue. All while I cut the cord, and stand up for what I knew. It was part of a task that was unravelling the truth. I fell into a dead end, facing another trace in the end. I had to make do, for what was done, for it was way to extensive way overdone.

So, when the time come; I could feed off the outcome. For all I knew it was all in my head. I was left to repeat; rebel and press delete. Because it was part of a sure thing, I was given an opportunity to return hit back and win. where the rest will follow and the corrupt will have swallow their pride.

For repeating an everlasting meeting to get in, will bring forth a new chapter. All so I can catchup and win another inning. I had to feed off the corrupt, all while I remain sturdy, warned of what to come from that outcome. I was torn in more than one direction fighting back another resurrection.

It had me rise above and follow through on another review. Just to get a glimpse of a future event. For what I saw before me; was an absolute threat. I could not find solace; it gave me a chance to hit back in advance. When I reached the end the only thing that was standing was an error.

It had me withstanding another trace, to that case. It caused an effect and brought me a further, closer to where I am meant to be because those who knew wanted to face me hit me and run break the silence and feed off the outcome. A challenge that served me well; saved me, before I fell.

I fell into a debt a finally before I hit the end of that threat. A spellbinding feast that had me face another trace. It was part of a trick, that caused an effect and broke the silence so I can resurrect. A treat, that brought me forward. It took me on a trace that had me hit back and fight another case.

A final defeat to that delay that had me face another bad day. Where I get in, face another inning. Feed off that trend, that had taken me in and broke the intension from within. It had me face another resurrection. Where the end result forced me to hit back with a warning.

Where the corrupt knew, took over that review with no value. It lacked custom it forced its way through a trace that had me face another key at the end of that travesty. It reported me every time I hit the end of that trace. It took me in and went into viewership; for an ongoing win.

For they had no freedom, nor foundation to fight back. Because they already entered, hit me once over. Causing an effect that had me refined and forced to get back on track and defame another vision to the game. Now they were returning for a killing; this time around; the feast, back fired.

No time than the present no trace to erase. A challenge I could face had me on the red, it was part of a given a chance to break the trance that hit me in advance. For

I was given an interpretation to release damnation. So, when I reached the end of that trend the drama will unfold.

Where I am given a challenge that had me face another case. For the corrupt will no longer have the power to repeat, report and rebel against that spell. Because I fell into a trap that had me face another trace at the end of the race. It set me back caused an effect and pushed me off track.

I was holding a grudge it forced me to return the favour and hit the corrupt like no other. I was taught a lesson left to repeat and rebel against those who put me through hell. I was trapped in the middle of a trip down memory lane, facing the corrupt at the end of that train of thought.

Repeating another dead end, had me releasing a demon in the end. It forced me to pretend. It had me on the edge, raiding the heads of those who have attempted to get ahead. It was forcing me to release that beast that had me find peace. I was edge of returning the favour.

It warned me of what was to come from that outcome. Because I hit an ending before I had a chance to leave a mark. It had me face another trace force to repeat and replace. It had been pending for a while; every trend had become part of an expense that had me forced to hit back with remorse.

I was on the road to recovering every trace. It had me stirring the pot, hitting back with a curse you cannot reverse. It was the beginning of a never-ending channel.

It changed my perception it handed me a redemption it forced me to recreate a challenge that handed me it caused an effect.

It restored my energy and created a trend. It hit me with a curse that served me well at the end of that trend. It solved what I thought was curse to my Dynasty. In fact, it was part of a trend that had me regain conscious awareness again. It took me in and finalised what I thought was tormenting me.

It served me well handing me a presentation to face another foundation. Where every trace had me face another test to that conquest. It pushed me in the corner faced me at every finally. So, when I hit the end, the most I would get out of it was give in. Pretend and challenge the corrupt in the end.

I was given a reason to return for one more season. When the time come overcome a trend that had me facing a dead end. I was on the move wasting a trace to that case. It had me forced to hit back with remorse. I was taught a lesson, left to reminisce in the past; holding a guilt trip in the present.

I was taught a lesson left to repeat; a given a reason to face another treason. So, when I reached my pinnacle the only thing that held me back was the chaos that followed. I as given a trend, feeding of the dead end. When I reached the top, the trend that stirred the pot; gave me a chance to belt back.

Because that was the thing that held me back from within. It was part of the drama that followed. It was handing me the energy that took me forward straight into a dramatic effect that handed me a trial and error. Trapped in the corner for a turn to teach them a lesson had returned.

for a favour broke loose and I had to break the silence and hit back with a vengeance. Because every time I hit back, there would always be a setback. Where I was stuck trying to catch up and face another trace at the end of that case. A given momentum to hit back at the end of that trend.

Because I fell into a heap, straight out of the deep. Hell froze over; I was given the opportunity to belt the corrupt with scrutiny. It had me on a path that had me hit over and under. Where the corrupt were storing all their negativity towards my direction.

A case had a trend it had me Creating a foundation that will hand me a final result. It was hitting the corrupts Secret. A mystical occult, that had me face what I thought was the last resort, at the end of that demonic treaty. A foundation that handed me an evaluation and the end of that transition.

Became my position that brought me forward, it was handing the energy to restart a new adventure. I was on the case at the end of that race. Trying my hardest to harvest, For I was given the energy to repeat replace and put the corrupt through hell at the end of the race.

I needed to feed off the poison that handed me a final eruption. I had to follow up on a trend that had me succeed through the end of that lead. It served me a purpose that handed me an evaluation to that method. It forced me to hit back and face another case denying the corrupt access.

I had to follow up on a claim that had me remain vigilant to the game. It was part of a caution, where I was warned of what was to come from that outcome. I needed to face a trace at the end of the race. I had to follow up on a permission to lead the plot and face a brand-new ploy.

What I thought was part of an expense, had me reach my potential way too late. It forced to repeat then without knowledge, feed off the concept and hand me a trend that will break the silence and feed off the corrupt in the end. It had me wanting more and feeding off the corrupt with an encore.

I had to meet them half way, just to find I was heading towards heresy. I had to give in and rebel against their needs and wishes all the way. For the entrance was a maze, there were to many obstacles to overcome. An illusion to a communion that became part of the corrupts final game.

I was living a drama over my empowerment, just to succeed. There were several on my raider that wanted to see me fail. So, they presented me with a last laugh, hounding me at every draft. I was taken for a fool declined from repeating a disclosed event to an anomaly that handed me closure.

An annulment that handed me enduement. An overdue task, that was taken by the storm hit me at the end of that trend. It faced me with a curse I could reverse, all I had to do was rehearse face another trace. It had me break the cycle and feed off the energy that led me astray.

For the corrupts entrance had me facing another delayed restoration; to that manifestation. It caused an effect and gave me the energy I needed to release that beast. It took me for a fool and had me attend another dead end. It handed me the end of that quotation that served me well.

I was used to get in, left me suffering while they were winning. I was put on back burner, living in a challenge that had me on standby. I was to regain that game regret facing a neglect. Then when the time come, overcome that final feast. Where in the end of that trace, the challenge will erase.

I had to release peace, rely on the corrupts method to get by. I was given a challenge that served me well. It handed me an introduction to a follow up; that put me through hell. For the corrupt had given me the edge of reason replicating the next mission. A second trial, rewarding me with serenity.

Terrorising my spirit and facing me with a trial an error added with a final vendetta. It had made me on the edge sorting whom out, there were several who took me in and faced me with a brand-new development from within. It was facing a trace that gave me a chance to break the system.

I had to sweeten the deal and face another trend at the

end of that debacle. The one that traced and trapped me putting me through hell so they can stay afloat. For what I knew and to what I assumed would come true, gave me a second chance to hit back and follow up on a feast.

It had me reach my pinnacle and press delete. Put in a position where they had me under ransom, facing another trace to that case. It lined me up for a feast and a final adventure that cut that cord and faced me with a trial and error. Break the cycle face that test and hand the corrupt denial.

I hit a delay, returning for one more chance to press replay. I was pushed to my limits. I hit a downslide, facing the end of that trend that took me in and broke that feast that had me state a new fact waiting for the person who attacked me to get back on track.

I had to face another trend, at the end of that impact. It was way too hard to enclose for the method gave me the energy to hit back with synergy. It had me feeding off the corrupts method, waiting for the trace to release that beast. It had me facing another ending that was pending.

I had to face a disclosure, to that vision that handed me an abreaction. It was part of an interaction that created an internal investigation. Where the corrupts final resurrection became of a deception. It had me involved in an expense, that served me well at the end of that forthcoming spell.

It was part of a pointless affair that saw me easy. Then

wanted to face me with a challenge that did not come easy. I had to improvise follow up on a review give in to the corrupts method while I get in and challenge everything from within. It was part improvable event that made me suspectable.

It was part of a challenge that had me face another debt. For that imposter served me well at every spell. It was farfetched and it handed me a key that had me face another degree. where the corrupt were pushed in the corner attempting to pressed replay. Trapping the corrupt in the corner.

I was taught a lesson and left to pick up where I left off. Feeding off accession to that deliberation. A continuation to that manifestation. I was taken in and took me in and broke the silence from within. I had to break the cycle and feed off the trace that had me face another momentum.

The game was a trial an error and a repeat to that final era. As I rebelled against that forthcoming spell. The energy that failed me had me encouraged to face another trace. Forced to hit back with an impact. A dilemma that presented me with a key that served me well; it brought me back to reality.

In the end of that trend, I had to face another dead-end. A debacle that forced the corrupt to commit a crime. Then have to have them admit their trick confess that test. While I hand them a dead end at the end of that trend. Facing me at every bend, breaking the corrupts silence in the end.

It had me follow up on a trace, that served me well, an ending that caused an effect and brought me hell. I was taught a lesson; it gave me the power and the entrance to release that beast. Forcing me off the edge of reason. Creating an entrance to that manifestation that warned me I hit malfunction.

Because I was let down, way too many times the energy that served; brought me forward then deserted me. Hit way to early; it left me to repeating what I thought was a condition that handed me an introduction to the next mission. Forcing me to repeat and rebel against that forthcoming spell.

All while I catch up and catch the corrupt about to hit me run and finalise the outcome. For I was given a chance to hit back in advance. Before they could return and roughen me up the curse was reversed and I was given the opportunity to return and hit the corrupt with a final feast.

I was given a chance to delve into a trend, having me face a dead-end. The condition was memorable the trace was imperishable. In the end of that mission, I was given a chance to return for repetition. I was hit with a challenge that had me encounter a trace; at the end of the race.

When the corrupt returned they were back on track, handing me an evaluation to that manifestation. It caused an effect and had me resurrect face a fear and repeat after the fact. All so I can give in and feed off the trace that had me fast forward until the end of the race.

just so I can get back on track and rebel after he who put me through hell. For I was given an expense that had me face another trace at the end of that trend; that handed me a dead end. I was back on track given a free ride to outdo and follow up on another review.

I was left to repeat, face a trace handing the corrupt a division to that composition. Where I got in and was taught a lesson. It forced me off track handing me an evaluation. I needed to get back on track, catch a break cave in on the concept. It had me on the edge protecting my soul in the end.

I was up and ready, trying my luck to belt the corrupt. It was part of a trace that had me on the case. It had me on the edge repeating a competition; to that evaluation. Handing me the conformation I was stepping into unknown territory; waiting for the trace to end in tragedy.

A follow up to that break, had me face another trace. It forced me to repeat and replace a final destination to that manifestation. It was causing an effect at the end of that debt. I had to face another common ground. Landing me in an evaluation to that manifestation that caused an effect.

It brought me back to reality; where it had me kicking a fuss. I was given a reason to hit back with treason. My destination was beginning to look humble. Every trace had me forced to erase. It gave me a second trial to follow up on a review. I had no time than the present to evaluate.

For the truth was to set me free, it was to give me a chance to delve into my position. The one trace that had me face a trial and error. It had me feed off the mission and create a disposition to the corrupts proposition. It was handing me an evaluation, towards a destination; that levelled me up.

It was giving me an opportunity to rise above scrutiny. It was part of an entrance to a final, where I had to release that feast that was holding me to ransom. I felt as if I was in a hostage environment and those who knew could d not wait to fail me and leave me stranded right through.

CHAPTER 3

◆ ◆ ◆

DISCONNECT CORRUPT YOU OWE ME

It had me forced to hit back and face another feast. I was given an opportunity to rise above and beyond scrutiny. It broke the silence; I was taken advantage of. I was left to face another informal interrogation to that investigation. It handed me the foundation to repeat and rise above.

It led me towards a journey that had me face another test, at the end of that conquest. I was given a chance beyond that evaluation to that interrogation to face another vision to that transition. It had me forced to hit back break the silence to get me back on track. It had me on the edge of reason.

For I was taken for a fool, I hit an ending that was pending, it gave me a sense of release, knowing I was left to repeat report and face those who took me in and assumed they can return and belt me from within. I had to release that beast. that served me well. The one that forced me through hell.

It was handing me the interrogation that manifestation; putting the corrupt through an investigation. A journey that will help me stand out from the crowd and stick up for myself. Because I was led on it left me to remain vigilant to the game. Every opponent had me follow up on a review.

It served me well and presented me with upcoming spell. It had me face a trace; forcing me to repeat a beat to that drum. It was part of a trend that had been pending. It was a follow up on a dead end. Replacing a given, just to face the forbidden; an interaction from within that treason.

I had given the corrupt a chance to delve in to the end of one road. A beginning of a new venture. One that was troubling my mind; I could not give it my best shot. I was put on a path where I would get shot. I had to delve into a challenge that brought me forward; straight into a daze.

On a path that left me raiding the heads of those who harmed me. An assumption that hit me with a redemption at the end of that invasion. Walking towards a destination where I was given a challenge where the trace will become a trial an error. A failed attempt that handed me a vendetta.

The passion to destroy me became way to overpowering. I was stuck in the middle of a riddle only to witness I hit a rebuttal. I was taught a lesson, warned of what was to come after the fact. It gave me a second chance to hit back in advance. For every trial served me well and handed me denial.

My reality took over and I had to accept defeat. For in the end of that trend I was served well. The only thing that had me facing a trace was on trial. An error to that conspiracy that handed me an evaluation. It took me on a journey worse than I could imagine.

It had me on the edge, preparing me for another pledge. For I was taken for a fool at every momentum. It had me second guessing. I had to hit the corrupt with a challenge that served me well and presented me with an ongoing sentiment to that evaluation.

It had me facing an interrogation to that manifestation. It forced me to repeat and face me in-between. So, when I hit the end of that trend I will finalise the mission and compel against that stigma that put me through hell. For I had to unite with those who had me at hello.

Facing me with a picture-perfect momentum, I was led astray. It was handing me a proposition to lead me towards a destination that had me facing another investigation. Where I was taught a lesson every step of the way. For I was left to repeat and remain silent at every competition.

Where I was given a spurt of energy at the end of the mission. It was part of a trace, that forced me out of that trend right in the middle of a competition. I was put in a position that faced me with a proposition. It had me follow up at the end of the mission complying with some else's vision.

Failing me with remorse in the end of that cause of action. it had me following up on an entrance that had me face another trace. It was part of a reason, it made me wonder why I hit the wrong end of that method. A trend that had me remain silent just I can restart a new trace.

Because I returned and hit back with treason, there was no reason for me to state a fact. Because I had no foundation to push me off track. I had to give in and follow up on a trace that served me well at the end of that incantation. Because I was stuck in a time warp; spell bound.

It was handing me a curse that had me face another verse. For the formation. to belt the corrupt at every foundation had me trace a given destination haunting me at every resurrection. It gave me a chance to get back on track. For I needed to repeat and replace another trace.

It had me forced to cause an effect. It led me to a destination that had me resurrect. I hit the end of that trial and error. No longer terrified, but mortified for those who knew could not wait to screw me right through. It was forcing me to take charge and repeat a trip down memory lane.

It was handing the corrupt doubt and I a free ride to the other side. Warning whomever, the trace was part of a final vendetta. It was part of the drama that faced me with a final, another trace to hand me the evaluation to the next communion. A common trade that had me face another trace.

It was part of a clear road, to disclose the corrupts method. Leaving me troubled at the end of that trend. I was on the path to release that beast that had me face another feast at the end of that case. It handed me an evaluation to break the system and that cycle; that was harming me at every trial.

It caused an effect and presented me with an evaluation; at the end of that manifestation. For that door never remained idling. It was part of a challenge that served me well it gave me a second chance to put me through hell. It challenged me with a key; road to recovery.

For the trauma was part of a trace had me face another trend at the end. Where I felt trapped and triggered by a past offence. It had me face another trace, handing the corrupt a final vendetta to that tremor. It forced me to hit the end of that trend breaking the silence; a corrupts final reliance.

A trace at the end of that case, became superficial. It had me face another road, permitting me to follow up on a path that caused and effect and handed me an expense to help me resurrect. I had to trace, it back when. Then face another release to that beast that handed me a feast.

It had me presenting the corrupt with a challenge I cannot erase. It caused an effect; it gave me a second chance to follow up on what I thought was part of the corrupt. It was my way of accepting what I thought was defeat. In fact, I was about to hit with a challenge that had me delete.

It delayed every momentum and faced me at every evaluation. It had to face a trace, and follow up on a new improved journey all the way. I had a threat that ended in denial. Where everyone involved served me well and presented me with a forthcoming spell.

I had to regain conscious awareness, start again, feed off the concept that had me face a warning in the end of that yearning. For I was given a challenge that had me face another trace. It was part of an ending; that had me face another trend. A pending development that caused an effect.

I was led towards a trial and error; a final vendetta. For the trap brought me forward it took me in and gave me a second chanced to delve into a trend that served me well in the end. For he who knew took, tuck me in the corner and faced me with a trend; that handed me a dead end.

For what I thought was the last resort, was part a fellowship; It had me face another trace. It became part of the trend that was facing me with a dead end. So, when I reached my pinnacle, I could return and press delete. It had me on the edge wrapped up in a position worse than the mission.

Because the trace had no admiration just an exemption to the rule. An exaggeration to antagonise the mission pumped up the volume. It created a deception to the corrupts redemption. Once again superficial, because I developed too early. I wanted it all then and now; my patience ran thin.

I watched it all unfold, and collapse it led me to destination where I hit a relapse. I was with the notion I could indulge and encourage the corrupt to return for salvation. I was taught lesson left to return then when the time come undo another review.

All while I follow up on a trace that had me face another mission; to that competition. It was compelling at the end of that presentation. It had me warned I was given an expense that had me race to the finish line. I was waiting for the corrupt to return and erase that follow up.

I was on the edge; it gave me a proposal that served me well. What I thought was part of an expense, had me race to the finish line. For the image had me face another trace and break the trend. It was silencing the corrupt and handing me exposure. A need to break the corrupts silence.

In the end of that trace, I was given a permission to break the tradition. I had to belt the corrupt at the end of the race. In case I lost all desire to regain that indifference to the game. It had me face and erase that turmoil that took me in. I was faced with a trial and an error; from within.

In the end I had to erase, it was handing me a force I could hit back with. Because every trace served me well and broke the silence while it put me through hell. I had to face remorse, cave in on the concept and prepare myself for a feast. It served me well and handed me a release.

It forced me to repeat remain silent and press delete. I was taught a lesson, watched the corrupt unveil another trace to that sale. Where I was put in a position gaining wisdom at face value, to that evaluation. For it handed me the case, causing an effect and breaking the silence so I can resurrect.

Others were watching me peak, thinking of ways to face me and hit me with delete. I was sitting on a trend, that had me face a dead end. It lined me up for a feast that had me release peace. It had me on the edge, repeating a new trend. It was part of a theme, that held me hostage in-between.

I was given a trace it was part of a test that had me regress. I was on the mend leading the pact regaining consciousness and starting fresh. Giving me the impression I hit a brand-new theme, a concept that had me face a new scheme facing denial and a trial in-between.

I was taught a lesson, tested beyond repair, it left me to release that beast that forced me to find peace. It was part of an expense that had me face another expose. For every drama faced me with an ending that was pending.

A trace that was never ending. A challenge that had me surrender.

It forced me to redo and accomplish another clue. I had to keep up with the program and face one more review. It gave me a chance to hit back in advance; facing an avalanche. I was hitting a revue that had me under scrutiny, waiting patiently for the corrupt to overcome an outcome.

I was given an interview that took me on a journey that led me towards a faith less likely for me to evolve. It was part of a trend that laid the law and forced me to hit back with a boat that served me well. It faced me with ongoing spell. It was part of a challenge that had me repeat rebel.

A condition to the mission had me relying on the corrupt at every composed repetition. It had me face another mission that served me well and gave me a second chance to break the silence. I had return for one key it forced me to repeat and face a new case.

I was hit with a challenge that served me a key, it faced me and hit a brand-new reality. It had me face another case and led me towards a journey that served me a brand-new reality. It was stated that the trace was based on a condition; that handed me a repetition.

It forced me to repeat and re-appeal to the next competition. I was led to believe I had no faith nor reason to repeat. What I had was a vampire effect that had me repeat a trace at the end of the race. It was part of a trend at the end of that bend that took me for a reasonable threat in the end.

I was taken for a fool it gave me a second chance to delve into a method that served me well at the end of that upcoming release to that piece. It was part of a failed attempt, that had me wasting my time fighting off a new trace. It caused an effect and had me restore my energy at the end.

Warning me every time I was given a reason to recreate a trace. It will hand me the face that will break the cycle an evaluation that will have me face an informal investigation. It forced me to repeat and follow up on a brand-new decision that had me release that proposal.

I was given a reason to face another trace that will have return for one more case. Where in the end of that trend it will help me face a dead end. A competition that will give in forcing me to return repeat and face another trace at the end of that race.

For whatever come to recognition, handed me the evaluation that served me an investigation. Warning me the corrupt were covering up another mistake. Giving me the impression the challenge was nowhere near the incur. It was to interrogate and hand me a consignment; a final vendetta.

It had me restoring my energy in the end, feeding off my journey periodically. I was energised by the trace, claimed by my truth, all while given an opportunity to face another scrutiny. I was to get back on track and face an impact. I was handed a negative outcome, towards a task that served me well.

Where in the long run the journey will give me the power and the indication that every forced will break the silence and return for one more key. It passed me and gave me the energy to break the system push them in the corner and leave them suffering in sorority.

For I had to face another failed attempt to challenge those who had handed me doubt. It gave me the freedom to back down and face another force, all while I hit back with remorse. For that case had caused an effect and gave me the impression I had to review and follow up on another clue.

It was part of an entrance that had me entertained. A benefit that served me well and forced me to praise those who had the audacity to put me through hell. I was left to remain conscious taken to a path of deception. A willingness to hand me a road to recovery; a challenge that will serve me well.

I was restoring an energy that handed a chance to hit back in advance. Harvesting someone else's trace at the end of the race. Giving in; breaking the silence so I can get by. All by hitting the corrupt while I was sitting on standby. Restoring what I thought will give me a chance to hit back in advance.

A challenge that had me stepping into a trace. It served me well at the end of the race. An energy to validate what I thought will bring forth a trace, it had me trapped and accommodating an ending that was pending. A trend that was never ending. It created a vindictive natural habitual offence.

Just to get the corrupt to admit their failure. It forced me to repeat create a definite response. It had me feeding off the departure that hit me when I took it all in and restored my energy from within. The nature of the response had me facing another upheaval. Religiously fighting for a lost cause.

Ready to feed off the souls who fed off me whole. I had to catch a break feed off the intake, then when the time come return the praise with an expense that had me release that beast. It forced me to find peace just before I created a thread. Denying me access and breaking that trace.

It had me face a case, leading me to a destination. It had me follow up on a trend; an ending that was pending. For what I knew handed me a brand-new review. In hindsight I was stuck in the light, dumbfounded by the image; because the light was way too bright.

I was on the edge, of reasoning with the devil, hounding the coach then hitting the principal with a reminder. There was no siren no jinx no challenge to predict a future event. Because the corrupt saw the light and entered my realm; on the realization they were dealing with the Devil thy self.

The Demon from within and the devil you know had me face another win. Where the energy that had me face a race broke the system and forced me to repeat and rebel towards another forthcoming spell. One for the trace was part of a case that had me review that everlasting clue.

For that trend in the end was overpowering it gave me a second chance to hit back in advance warning me the error of that tremor became invasive and the only way out was the way in and even then, there was no entrance. Nor a stigma just a presentation to create an enigma.

CHAPTER 4

I CAUGHT THE CORRUPT HIDING A FLAW

Warn me no more, the task was a given handed to me friction. A prediction towards a long awaiting mission. The path I was on, was part of a challenge that kept me strong. An expectation long overdue, it had me face a case, feed off the trace. Presenting the corrupt with a failed outcome.

I hit fraud, found myself in a position that was part of a prediction that was interesting enough feeding off the corrupts proposition. An allegation that elevated to the next manifestation. A journey that had come my way, had given me a chance that served me well along the way.

I was presented with a trace, that served me the wrong case. It gave me the proposition, to hit back with an invasion, towards an interesting development. It was part of an accomplishment; facing a debt. For those who knew could not wait to return scheme scam and fail me in-between.

With a composition to that mission, I had to praise and follow up on another trade. It was part of trace that had me cave in on the concept in-between. I had to face a trace give in to the corrupts final case. When I reached the end of that pinnacle, the task that was pending; had me surrendering.

It had me facing the truth it became part of a trend that had me regain conscious awareness again. For the same game that had me facing another train of thought. It had me following up on another repetition at heart. An entitlement, where every violation warned me there was no chaos.

For that road of recovery had me facing a pathway that served me well. It presented me with ongoing spell. It was part of an entrance to the unknown, a curse I could reverse. I was given a chance to return and hit the corrupt back in advance. All while I come first, facing another curse.

It took me on a journey that faced me in advance. The last entrance to that method that forced me off the edge. I was returning the favour so I can get in and pledge. It was part of a given trend a challenge that will hunt me down and face me with a trace; in the end of that forthcoming event.

I had to walk in and follow up on a new praise; served me well. I had to face a trace, protect myself from a free ride to other side. An entitlement that served me a curse I cannot rehearse; unless I return and reverse. Because every trace had a case and every road hit me with a warning.

It served me a desire to fight back and break the system back on track. For the only thing that come my way was the last thing that served me well from within. For those who saw me as an easy target restored their energy and fed off me; when I hit and ending that was pending.

That stagnant affair, affirmed the obvious. For what I knew, gave me the power to undo; what the corrupt were planning to do. Creating a war in their peace all while facing a brand-new feast. It had me on the edge creating a new trace, preparing me for an entrance that will break the silence.

I had to examine and study every momentum. Not only I was stuck trying to comfort myself from a challenge that had me cave in on a win. But it gave me a second chance to repeat rebel and follow-up on another spell. It pushed me in the corner faced me with a trend.

It served me a sentence and broke the silence; it had me face another endeavour. It had me following up on a vendetta. With the notion I had no freedom to fight back, it served me a trace that had me get back on track.

By the time I was served a clue the corrupt saw me as an easy target.

It faced me with a final review, a challenge that that had me second guessing. It served me well and got me through. Tracing that method and forced me to return with the same old game. Waiting for the corrupt to take the Bait. Then when the time come face another outcome.

For what they knew, and what they were attempting to achieve was an absolute joke. It had me face another trace; it led the pact and created a definition to get back on track. because they were given permission to release all inhibition, they had me face another review.

It had me follow up on a key that served me well. It presented me with an ongoing spell. For the situation created a follow up to the next road. A journey that had forced me to repeat another drive to the other side. For that curse had me rehearse it forced me to face another trace.

In the end there was a case, ready to be replaced. A trend that had me face another dead end. I was trying my luck to get back on track and trap those who used me to get in; reassuring me I will never win. Assumed that their method will bring them peace. But all it did was create war in my peace.

For I was on the move guessing wrong finalising the impression and creating a long line of negative effects. An effort to break the trace and heave at the train of thought that had me face another trend. It had me breaking the system and starting again. I had to face a trace and protect my soul.

It had me from that feast on a trace that created a trend that served me a dead end. Where every challenge gave me a final review. It served me well, broke the silence that put me through hell. I had to cave in the trend that forced the corrupt to return for a dead end.

Then when the time come face another outcome. Where every piece, brought me forward. It had me trace another trend at the end of that test; that caused an effect. It led me to erase that key that served me periodic test. A trace that forced me off the edge straight into a ditch.

It was part of a curse, that had me come first. A challenge that served me a piece, returned for one more release. For the favour that faced me with a curse had me follow up on a thread that had me tread lightly. Just so I can return and start again. Torn in every direction; where it taught me a lesson.

I had to face another trace, create a piece, and force myself to release and find peace. So, when I reached my pinnacle the only thing that had me held me back was the curse I could reverse and the trend that served me well and brought me forward straight out of hell.

I had to follow up on a faith, cancel out what I thought was the last resort. I was given a trend that served me well in the end. It brought me forward and broke that system that took me in and fed off the challenge that trapped me from within. A trace that had me play it the way the corrupt wrote it.

It gave me a second chance to hit back in advance. I was forced to reveal a trend at the end of that dead end. It took me on a path that had me face another trace. It caused an effect and forced me to hit back with a final request. For I was left to repeat escape with a trend in the end of that trace.

It had me replace a case with a dead end in the end of that trend. I was given a chance to hit back in advance, forced to hit an enigma to that stigma. I was led on, trapped in a space that had me face a trend at the end of that final failed free ride. Towards the other side of that trace; have me subside.

I was on the edge of reason warned of what was to come from that trace. It had me face another case. It was putting me in a position worse than I could imagine personally attacking me at every destination. It had me face a trace giving me permission to return for one more competition.

In the end it was pausing effects, feeding off the vision; that brought me a composition. It gave me a second chance to state a fact cause an effect and feed off the impact; that got me back on track. I was led on, and left to remain silent, to a game that was chasing the blues away.

It had me face a trap, that had me afraid to fight back. I was not aware at the time those whom trapped me in their world had me feeding them joy. They had me locked in, while they were reaping rewards leading me to a destination; never to see light. I lose full power, no vision to empower.

I could not enter any realm; that will find me well. I had no choice, but to rejoice, curl away in my own world. It had me racing to the end of that trend and breaking the silence so I can pretend. For the demons in my head took over. The only thing that had me space out in between was the truth.

Preventing me of returning for another yearning. I had to fight back, contaminate the corrupts mission; just so I can get back on track. For the condition I was handed branded me. It gave me the trace that served me well at the end of the race. I was on the mission to get back what was stolen.

It was a given to release that beast. I was on track and finalise the competition to rely on no one to get by. Because I knew in truth, no one could help me; unless I gave in. It handed them a chance to break my spirit from within. It had me waiting for me to fail; so, I never reach my Holy Grail.

I was stuck in a time warp, fighting off a Demon that forced me to win. He who entrapped me took me in and faced me with a terrible lie; so, I never get in. The fact I was led on, towards a break that had me fake a false reading. I was forced to repeat replay, trap the corrupt in the corner all the way.

It gave me another chance to fight back and press replay. I had to break the corrupts silence and uncover up their mission; all so I can get back on track. So, when the time came; I was trapped no longer in the same domain. For the trace had come to an end, breaking the chain; I remained simple.

No more mission to accompany me to a dead end. No validation to that manifestation, where I had to undo and follow up on another review. No tread to raid my head, I had to follow up on a key that forced me to repeat. Trace and trick the corrupt so they never return and face me with the same.

For he who knew, had me face another case. I was given a reason to hit back with treason. For the trend had pushed me in the corner. It was part of a given momentum, served well and presented with a foundation to release the beast; following up on a new piece.

I was faced with a case that had me follow up on a trend in the end. It had me face a trace, tested way too many times. I was taught a lesson and left to embrace in one more case before I cause an effect handing me the energy to face another trace get back on track and feed off the impact.

It forced me to return and face another trace. Where I was under the impression the game was part of a gamble that served me well. I was handed an extension to that redemption that took me further. It handed the corrupt a final reservation to that damnation.

It presented me with a curse; I could reverse. All I had to do was return the favour, and follow up on a review. It was part of a final interrogation, to finalise the investigation. Where I was given opportunity to prove I was innocent. It had me face another trace where I took advantage of it.

It was purely for me to catch up, and close an argument. Not lose a fight at this point of time. I was interrogated against my named was tarnished and I could feel it all unfold. I was left to play a plot that had me gambling my dream away. Terrorised and pausing effects.

I was in terrible shape, because of it. It had me in a position that Left me sit in a presentation that had me facing an investigation. Forced to hit back with a charge, a duty of care, that will have me stalling. Long enough to repeat it at a later date. Meanwhile the corrupt win every fight.

It had me facing a trial a lead that had me living in denial. If I gave them the opportunity, to rise above that scrutiny that handed me unity. I was a given a reason to declare and disclaim another scare. Leading me to a destination that will have me reach my limit without restrictions.

My state of mind overstimulated, I was left hitting a trend that had me forced to hit a dead end. I was forced to hit back and face another experience. It had me develop a case that returned at hit me at the end of the race. It was part of a trend that had me face a dead end.

I was stuck in a rut, others who knew could not wait to screw me right through. The instigation became an interrogation; it forced others who had a clue; attack me right though. It left me to suffer in silence while the attacker's live life to the fullest. Forced to hit back with remorse.

Faced with a journey I could reckon with, a given opportunity to state a fact. Face a trace and create an impact that will embrace that case. A given impression I hit the end of my wither, handing the corrupt bad weather. Meanwhile feed off the trace that handed me the empowerment.

I needed to entrap another trend, at the end of that presentation. It gave me the power to release and devour. With every prize there was always an enterprise. It had me face a case that served me well. It gave me the closure I needed to put the corrupt through hell.

It created a challenge that had me face a trace to that case. It caused an effect and broke the cycle so I can resurrect. As a result, it had me fall for a lie fail to get by. It handed me the ending that was pending and a trend that had me face an allegation that served me well.

Where every manifestation, that I endured took me on. It locked me in a pathway that served me wrong. Trying to remain strong and clearing the road had me face one more obstacle. Those who knew forced me to renew and follow up on another overzealous review.

The method was pungent and the energy stringent, it was stringing me along. Forcing me to hit back and face another trace at the end of the race. I had no freedom to empower or the power to devour. What I had was an extension to that redemption that took over my mission.

It forced me to hit back with admiration. It had me stagnant, long enough to break the corrupts spirit. For there was a string of events that had me on the edge of reason. I was accomplishing a goal and feeding off the trace that had me hit with treason.

It got to the point, where I had no faith, and the only thing left; was the troubles left behind. It had me reach my pinnacle facing another trace, at the end of the race. I was left to accompany the worse, encourage the best, get back on track, and feed off the stress.

A trace of energy, that was holding me to contempt. I was held hostage left to repeat forced to embrace feed off the trace. I had to find peace encourage my spirit to release. It had me on the edge to release and follow up on a feast. It had me release the beast catch up and face another trace.

I was warned of what was to come from that final outcome. I had to force my way in, and hit back with a challenge that warned the corrupt I had no freedom to win. The messages were going back and forth and the trailer to that method had me face another final.

A vendetta that handed me resentment had me face another trace. I had to acclaim a division to the game. It was part of a result to regain what I thought was part of a trend that had me face a dead end. I had to gamble that final review, sitting pretty; expecting my journey to release that beast.

It had me hit a dead end, that forced me to repeat. All while I replace and follow up on a journey that brought me back to reality. It was the beginning of a brand-new adventure a trace that served me well and presented me with an ongoing spell. The trend was pending and a trace never ending.

I had no challenge to release no foundation to find peace. What I had was an upcoming event that brought me a serious consequence to upcoming threat. a trace that served me well and presented with a faith that had me forced to release a beast just to find peace.

It took me in and broke the silence from within. There was no trend and the follow up to that method broke the silence and started again. I had to pretend that the energy that faced me became unworthy in the end. I was taught a lesson left to repeat; what I thought was the last resort.

I was warned of the consequences of the action of those who returned for an inspection. It had me face another stagnant affair. I had to free myself from a presentation that validated that investigation. So, I can give in and face another affirmation from the heart.

For whatever come way, the reason had me face another treason. The trend was pending the trap was never ending. The urge to return for one more hit, had me escape facing a demon, a final dream; hell of a nightmare in between. A thread to that junction that belted me with redemption.

An impersonator validated what I knew; caused an

effect. It had me breaking the decision to that redemption; it had me facing the wrong admission. A trend that had me face a dead end. A method that saw me fit and thought the next best thing was to hit me and break my spirit from within.

CHAPTER 5

◆◆◆

WHEN THE CORRUPT A FORCED TO SURRENDER

I, on other end multitasking asking for anarchy; for I was taken for a fool. I was left to remain vigilant to a game that had me on the edge; gambling my dream away. On the other end of that trend, once again, warned. The trace was about to be heaved, embracing the truth; with one more case.

I was given an extension to that validation that forced me to repeat and break the silence at the end of that trend that took me in and had me reach my potential from within. I was taken for a journey that had me reach my potential. Return the favour every time I was handed a list of demands.

I had no freedom to speak my mind, for the foundation was disembarked. I was on the edge of dissembling a pledge and nowhere near the dream, the trace was uncanny in-between. I was given a final endeavour and that was to hit back and feed off the trace; it had me embrace a vendetta.

The challenge that gave me the choice had me face another case at the end of the race. It was meant to be because the challenge, I was handed was embraced by the case that was open long ago. Enchanted by a key that took me by surprise and threw me off the raider straight into a trader.

A double agent, who had the motive to sustain pretended he was part of the game. It gave me a chance to delve into a trance led me to believe that the energy was part of the game. It caused an effect and brought me forward. I fell, repeating another forthcoming spell.

It was giving me the opportunity to remain silent. So, when the time come, I could overcome what I thought was part of the outcome. It was serving me well it had me facing another spell. A challenge that will keep me silent ready to revive a trace at the end of that case.

It caused an effect and presented me with a validation. Purely to remain strong at the end of that long holdup. Because I was handed a lie to get by the force that hit me with remorse caused an effect. I had no choice, but to return and hit back with a vendetta; a long awaiting one.

A follow up on a game, that served me wrong; when it was meant to serve me right. It forced me to repeat rebel and remain strong all while my adrenalin was running thin. I had to face another case feed off the trends that had me repeat rebel and start gain. It was all part of a given oppression.

I was mistreated on purpose, for those who knew had me as an easy Target. An impression that was created by peace. A trace that had me face a key; it gave me a chance to release that demon that forced me to repeat and follow up on a trace that stirred the pot and faced me with a challenge.

All while I get in and chase that win. A trace that returns for another sustained forbidden unreliable sin. All while I wash rinse a cleanse that long forbidden approach. It was long overdue and I was on the edge hunting down those who pledge. For whatever was left behind; never meant a thing.

There was always a trace that had me forced to replace, for that deception pushed me forward out of my comfort zone. It was handing the corrupt a loss not a redemption. It was harming them periodically, handing them the wrong end of that trend. Lining me up for a dead end.

It was the only pathway, where I could return hit back remain idling and start again. Feeding off the tremor and repeating a dilemma that had me face another tremor. I was trapped in the middle of a trace a tremor ready to dive in to shallow waters. Forced to hit back with honours.

By the time I hit the end of that lie, I was given an opportunity to hit back with unity. I was to give the corrupt a chance to get by. For every trace served me wrong and handed me an expense that had me forced to remain Just long enough to feed off the lie.

There was a trace that had me face another case. It forced me to repeat follow up on a trend that had me caged once again. I had to repeat and then report against the corrupts encore. For the trace became a trend, that had me face a dead end, at the end of the race.

It was part of a faith, less likely to erase and a trend that forced me to pretend. I had to invade in the privacy of those who held me up. For the energy that created a trend, served me well in the end. I had to sacrifice a new challenge it had me overlook a nook and a new outlook.

For the old took over the new and the edge of reason face me with treason. For the old took over the new and I had to face the facts. So, when I hit the end of that trend the game had made no sense. There were no troubles that could not be resolved, no trace that could not be erased.

For the challenges that had me face a case caused an effect and gave me the impression that the only thing that was left had me pause for one more threat. It had me face another trend in the end of that dead-end. It was part of a passageway towards a release that had me follow up on a feast.

I had to find peace then undo what I thought was the last resort. Where the only thing left was to betray and hit the corrupt with a bad day. A trace that had me face another dead end. It had me involve, another vague trade, and invade in a feast that forced me to release and find peace.

I had to feed off the trade, that forced me to embrace another trace. It had got to the point I had to release fight back and find peace. Just to get a glimpse of a final vendetta a challenge that served me well and put me through hell presented with an upcoming spell.

Where in the end, I was to get in and win then try my luck and feed off those who used me to get in. It was part of an energy that led me towards scrutiny. It was not allowing me to lead; they kept pushing me off the edge just so I do not breath. It got to the point I lost my way.

The only thing that served me well, was the troubles that forced me through hell. I had to catch up face another trace from within. I had no time than the present to undo and walk alone. It was part of a journey and a work load well done. I was over loaded with information not worth living.

I had no time than the present to hand the corrupt an independent evaluation. For that invasion had me lose my vision. There was no deception nor decision, just a trace that will hand me an impulse to that imposition. The assumption was not final; there was no freedom just an unresolved mission.

It was actually my chance to hand me redemption. It gave me a chance to invite them in all so I can catch up and feed off the trace that had me face another win. It was part of a test at the end of that request. My entrance to get in and harm their method from within; my way of accepting defeat.

An assumption hinting to whomever, will hand them a chance to trap me in advance. It was preventing me from repeating a new meeting. Providing me with an entrance to a pathway where every journey was handing me a line-up of treasure with undeniable measures.

It had, me lingering to the next theme where every trace had become part of a case that lined me up with a feast that served me well and presented me with an upcoming spell. Where I get in, and restore my energy from within. I had to reserve the right to acclaim a division to the game.

It had me gambling the corrupts trend, at the end of that final bend. It was part of a pointless affair that stabbed me in the back leaving me trapped ready to pull a string reap a reward and feed off the energy that forced me to repel and rebel against those who faced me and put me through hell.

It had me stating a fact, packing up, and leaving it to chance. Right before I was tested and taught a lesson once more. What chance did I have if I did not take a moment and advanced that trance, at the end of the race. Where every final vendetta brought me a final faith.

A presentation that led me to that investigation, brought me forward. The decision to harm me at every proposal had me casting a spell. It was feeding off the corrupts method while I went through hell. The decision of what end will encourage me to pretend was unprecedented.

I had to acclaim and accomplish a goal to break the cycle and remain solid. Not undone at the end of that outcome. Where in the end I was taught a lesson, giving me the impression I was let down and forced to face a trace at the end of the race. Embracing the true meaning of that cause of action.

I decided what end to take and what trace will partake that everlasting trend at the end of that what I thought was part of the last resort. in the end of that trend. For the energy that restored my every motion had me facing another wrong move at the end of that trend.

It brought me forward, led me to believe that every dream had a momentum. It was based on a journey that will come a reality and bring forth clarity. I had to do was focus on a foundation and the rest will follow. Even though the journey was a no show; every trace had me face a case.

The trace had come to a holdup it gave me a problem that served me a purpose. It had me face a trick that served me well. It hit me just before I fell into a trap that faced me with a trend that put the corrupt through hell. Little did I know that little white lie took me in and threw me off the edge.

Leaving me facing a dead end and death threat that forced me to portray another trade at the end of the day. For that division had me devoting my mission to the wrong opposition. It had me face a lead to the end of that stagnant affair that significant in the corrupts final despair.

It warned me I hit the end and every trend saw me visible. I was given a free ride to override a trade that served me well giving me the impression that served me an opposition caving in on the concept and breaking the silence that served me well at the end of that trend.

I was trying my hardest to disclaim and follow up on another game. Where the end of that dead end, it handed me a proposition that forced me to present the corrupt with a competition. It had me face a case and force me to get in and feed of the trauma; that broke the silence from within.

At the end of that breakable feast, I was given an impression to hit back with treason. I was left to state a fact break the cycle; to get back on track. I had no reason to face another treason. What I had gave me the impression the deception was worse that the illusion that served me restitution.

For I was given a feast to repeat and follow up on a trace at the end of the race. It was part of a game that led me astray straight into a development that kept me strong. A given reason to follow up on another treason, For I was handed a key a follow up to the next competition.

It was handing me an evaluation towards a destination that served me well. For I was left to state a fact feed off the impact and present the corrupt with another challenge. I was given a reason to catch up and finalise that trend that had me hit a dead end. It became part of an impossible task.

It served me well forced me through hell; it gave me a second chance to delve into a broken system. It brought me forward, it took me on a journey that trapped me in advance, it cleared my intuition. Led to regain conscious awareness again. An impossible task that had me face another trace.

It was feeding off the system at the end of the race. It had me face a trend that was part of a pointless affair in the end. It turned against me refined waiting for me to rely on whom ever to get by. It was facing a trend that took me into a violation; facing a competition to that mission.

It gave me a second chance to solve an issue; it had me feed off the trace that had me face a case. I was taught a lesson that led me to repeat, I had to undo a retouch another clue. I had to embrace release that beast force the corrupt to return for one more feast.

Relying on whomever to get in, had me face a broken system; that failed me from within. I had to step in to the ghetto, take a gamble, feed off the rest that had me face a conquest. It created havoc faced me with a feast; a test to that conquest. All while I get back on track, feeding off the impact.

I was given a reason to repeat, replace and face another pace; at the end of the race. Space it in between the old the new and the edge of reason, just so I can catch up and feed off the treason. Where I was stepping into the unknown, tormented by the truth and led to believe otherwise.

For those rumours, had changed; and the only thing that come my way had me guessing wrong and pressing replay. It was the entrance to another bad day. For the truth will set me free, it will give me ace of base and the power undo what I thought was part of an ongoing review.

I had a test it was part of a trip down memory lane. I was about to have the corrupt confess case that trace and feed off the mission that brought me an entrance that entertained me with the notion the corrupt had me face another condition to that mission that forced me to oppose a final.

It gave me a second chance to break the cycle and start a new refined clue. It was part of a trace that started with a glimpse. It caused an effect and had me face another trace. It was to catch up feed off the corrupt and face me with another release to that beast that had me stalling.

I was about to cause an effect, step into the unknown. It had me freshen up and erase another trace at the end of the race. It gave me the power and the energy to erase test that had me finalise that conquest at the end of that trend that served me well; warning me I just went through hell.

Reaching my pinnacle with a trace that served me well, taught me a lesson. It gave me a second chance to hit back in advance, forcing the corrupt to return with a yearning. It had me face another trace, at the end of the race. For the second chance to set it all up, at once set me free.

It made me see the light; it had me undo whatever had caused the wrong effects. Because I was given a reason to hit back with treason the validation that served me a wrong moved forward and the lie kept it strong. In the end it caused an effect and brought me forward straight into a defect.

I had to give in feed off the trend that served me well in the end. I was led to believe that the dream took over the Drama and the trace forced me to return and replace it with an investigation. It took me on a journey of a validating the truth. Where I had to cause an effect and challenge the concept.

A force to repeat had me step into a challenge to compete. I had to compel follow up on a forthcoming spell. It was part of a trace that served me well. It had me relinquishing, what I thought was the last resort. Caved in on the concept restored my energy too.

I took a moment and fed off the synergy. That forced me off the edge straight into a journey that led me towards a key sentiment. An exact momentum faced with a key that had me head strong, ready to repeat rebel holding on to a forthcoming spell. It led me to restrain finalising that mission.

Whatever remained the same, handed me the motivation to disclaim another competition. I was on the other end, facing a trend where in the long run. The corrupt were invading in my privacy, facing me with a new curse. Creating a trend that will challenge me and regain conscious awareness again.

It had me state a fact, forcing me to give in and repeat another tact. A curse where the corrupt cannot reverse because every journey I chose handed me an extension to that redemption that forced me to redo and repeat another competition. I had to keep up with the program.

I had to face a trace, give into the momentum. Restoring my energy without failure. Because the corrupt were forcing me to hit back with a creative trend. It was breaking my system and feeding off the mission so I can start again. For every trace had a case and every curse had a verse.

Where everything I did caused an effect and trapped me at the end of that threat. It served me well and forced me to return for one more chance to get through hell. A faith that had me return and follow up on another review. I was to hit back and present, the corrupt with a dead-end.

Pushing them off track straight in to an internal investigation. Creating a piece at every final allegation. I was given a solution to a journey that had me state a new fact. It was part of a trend less likely to reprieve. For that sentimental evaluation, had me harming the corrupt at every destination.

So, when I hit the end of that trend, the case will close and I will start again. Where the only thing missing was a dead end. A game with a gamble that had me step into the unknown. Haunting me from within waiting for the unjust to detach, then refresh; restarting.

CHAPTER 6

◆ ◆ ◆

WHEN ALL ELSE FAILS

I was on the brink, starting a new venture, where the corrupt were on the other end creating a new trace in the end. They had me face another trace trapping me at every race. Heaving at me at every centre. It gave me a chance to set it all free and face me with another unity.

The release to that demon was a knock on the door. It had me waiting, for the edge causing an effect and presenting me with a curse that served me well. It had me face another fear that trapped me in the end of that trend. It gave me a second chance to delve into a warning that had me start again.

I was given a reason to hit back with treason. It served me well and forced me through hell. The rough spot just to get a glimpse of a trace that took me in and fed off me from within. I had to cause an effect and state a new fact where every reaction pushed me off track.

I was taught a lesson left to remain silent, so when I hit the end, I could only pretend. For that trend had me face a trace. It was part of a method that forced me to return the favour, accommodate that interest and follow up on another lead. One where the corrupt lose and they cannot breathe.

It had me forced to hit back with remorse. A challenge that had me curse that verse chase that trace feed off the trauma and face another case. Where the only thing left was the game that had me wonder what I had to endure to break the system and face another blunder.

Where the edge of reason, caused an effect forced me to resurrect. Because I hit an ending where every trace led me off the trend straight into a dead. Where I was misunderstood, left to embrace another trace and follow up on a condition that had me erase that mission.

It was presenting the corrupt with a final opposition. No disguise to their intention, for they invaded my privacy and gave me the freedom to hit back with a warning. It was part of a trace that hit me with treason. It led me to danger in the end of that game; a chance to belt the corrupt all the same.

I was on the game hitting a second chance in advance.

A free ride that hit back with redemption in the end of that trace. It served me a curse at the end of that verse. I was taught a lesson to hit back with redemption. For they would have a forced me to heave; unbreak a trace at the end of the race.

Where I was taught a lesson, it gave me a challenge that had me case close that trap. It left me high and dry forcing me to hit back with a trace that had them get back on track and follow up on a faith less likely to for me to break the journey periodically; at the end of that blend.

All while I feed off the redemption that had me face a proposal. A fake and false deception to that validation that left me hit another waste; at the end of that case. In the end of that exposure, it had restored my energy taking me in and feeding off the drama from within.

I had to face a fear, one that had the corrupt forcing me to erupt. It had me on the edge reaping rewards and feeding of the concept a competition that had no remission. For whom I was competing with had no entry all they had was a trap that forced me to endeavour to devour at every hour.

A trace at the end of the race, caused an effect. It gave me the impression; I hit a deception to that redemption. It was part of misdemeanour that had me on the edge; facing another warning in the end of that theme; that had me face a dead end. I was given a free ride to embrace a trace.

It led me to play the game that had me face another bad

day. For that case led me to believe that the drama was too hard to perceive. I had to face a trace a given reason to belt the corrupt for no reason. I was taught a lesson, left to display and relay whatever challenge come my way.

The trace warned me in the end of the race. It was part of a condition that laid the law. It broke me at every encore. It was part of a trace that had me traumatized. Leading me towards a challenge that broke the silence. It had me temperamental forced to return; embrace a case and let it go.

All while I face a brand-new encore. A presentation that had me undo another review. It was forcing me to cover up another stagnation to that manifestation. It faced me with another warning at the end of that theme; that broke the silence in-between. For the corrupts method was part of a given.

It had me guessing wrong, trying my luck to remain strong. So, when I hit the end of the game that trace and the trend remained the same. For the trend had me face a deadened it gave me a faith that led me towards a journey that had me undo review and follow up on another clue.

For the game was a gamble, a trace that was part of a case, it had me verifying truth so I can take a moment to follow up on a trace and find peace at the end of that lease. I had to release that trend at every damnation. I was given a portfolio and an extension to that redemption.

It led me towards a journey that stated a fact. It gave me a chance to catch up and get back on track. It was part of a trace that had me face another case. It kept me simple ready to hit back and face another impact. It had me on the edge enduring to those who were insightful.

They were trying to catch up and face another trace, giving me the impression I was about to be hit a turn around. Where every trace took me on a path that had me face another case. It had me forced to hit back with remorse. Where I was given impression, I was to face another redemption.

Where every trend had me on the edge, of reason. It had me starting fresh, giving me the impression I was left to break the system. It had me feeding off the trace that had me replace a case. An ongoing catastrophic event that had me return the favour repeating another dead end.

It had me cause an effect, create a piece, trace that trap that led me off track. For every trend had me face another trace. It had me return for one more trap, it was part of a challenge that taught me well and pushed me of the edge, straight into a disaster that led me to repeat and repel.

It was handing me a brand-new adventure. It had me face another trace, it forced me to hit back and renegade, just to catch up and face a trace that had me convey another con corrupt mission the one that hit me at the end of that contraption. The drama was working against me.

I had so many on my raider waiting to fight me. It led me towards an investigation that had me reveal what I already knew. It was part of a challenge that had me face another trace. There was a competition that took me in and had me return the favour from within.

It was part of a conspiracy, that had me release that beast. It forced me to undo and trap those who knew, then repeat another review just soi can find another outlook to that refined trace to that case that caused an effect and broke the silence at the end of that threat.

It was time I returned and gave the corrupt a chance to release that beast. It had me follow up on another feast. Where this time around, I had freedom to face a feast, for the corrupt had me cornered, trying their luck to follow up on another affair.

Trapping those who were driven where they had me, eradicate another internal investigation. It led me to believe that every trend, had me face another dead end. I was given a chance to hit back in advance. It Gave me a case that had me reform to the next investigation.

For the energy that forced to review another overview, had me step into the unknown. It caused an effect and faced me with a threat and a flare in the air. I had to find a way out of that doubt that had me face a trace. It led me towards a direction of foul play; A challenge that will hand me a case.

I had to cease the day, follow up on another stagnant affair. It was part of a journey that led me to skip that trip down memory lane. I had to repeat press replay and delete just to catch up on a lead. I had to cancel my plans because I was led on and left to break that cycle in the end of that trend.

I was given an impression, a challenge that had me hit a redemption. It was handing the corrupt a final investigation. I had to face another trace and follow up on a feast that led me to believe that every truth had forced me to hit back with remorse. It faced me with a trace; a follow up on a cause.

Where every legal document was forged; forcing me to release that beast. It had me refine at the end of that trace that served me well. It gave me the impression I was led towards heaven and pushed through hell. Facing a revival to that piece; handing the corrupt a survival technique.

For that trap led me on, it trapped me in the end of that case. For the end of that host heaved at me at every arrival. It had me ceased creating a war in my peace. A case that had me release that beast forced me off the edge straight into a pledge. Breaking the cycle and leave me for dead.

I was to face my fear and lead the corrupt to a dead end in the end of that trend. So, when I least expect it, hit them with a final warning. I had start anew affair for the Horizon became part of a prediction. A journey that brought faith to that trend that failed me in the end.

It brought me forward, planting a new seed. Just to bring me a good deed, I had to tamper with notion there was no faith worth the commotion. Because I was left returning the favour, it had me forced to release that beast that faced me at the end of that lease.

It had me disadvantaged, causing the wrong turn of event. It that saved me periodically in the end. A trace towards a follow up on that served me well and presented me with a feast just to find justice of the peace. I was forced to repeat and give in to those who endanger me from within.

It was giving me the power to undo, and face a review, then follow up on a trend. All while I create a trace. It was part of a tradition, that will inform me of what to expect at the end of that lease. I had to release, poison that piece that earned me exposure. For my existence handed me an expense.

I was taught a lesson, left to release and create a resistance to that piece. It was pushing me forward at every distance. It had me create a trial an error and a final vendetta. I was given the impression that the exposure was invalid. In fact, it was part of the deal reminding me I was being stalked.

Stabbed in the back, left to give the corrupt a chance to get back on track. It had me step into a trace that led me to face another case. It caused an effect, that warned me I hit a threat and a dead end to that presentation that had me faced with a trace that served me well at the end of the race.

I had to release that feast that had me forced to find peace. It was part of a delay that handed me an opportunity to press replay. So, when I reach my destination, I could focus on what was holding me back. Then when without fail cut the cord, get back on track; creating a hollow effect.

It was part of a partition, to push me off my mission. All so I never make it to the next destination. I was to catch up, fight back then return to get back on track. Release that beast that had me face another feast a case that forced me to rely on whom ever to get by.

All while I try my luck and feed off the trace that had me face another case. For it gave me a chance to hit back in advance. It had me on the edge wasting that energy that had me face another trace at the end of that case. It was part of a trend that led me off the bend; straight into a dead end.

It was part of a piece that had me face another case, returning for one more release. A yearning to save myself from another trend. It had me passionately reviving another dead-end just to find peace from that release that had me facing another feast at the end of that lease.

I had to save myself from a chaotic feast, an event that had me face another trace at the end. For I was given an opportunity to release that beast that served me well at the end of that lease. It created a chance to catch up break the silence and hit the corrupt with a final alliance.

I had to face a trace, hit back with a cause of effect. An action that had me follow up on an abreaction. For what I thought was part of a trace to get back on track. Gave me a second chance to reserve the right to break the silence and hit back with a final bite.

A turn of events that had me under scrutiny. It was part of a trend that served me well in the end. I had to face another trace curse another verse feed off the energy that handed me the monarchy. It was part of a faith that left me erratic in the end of that trade. I was tied up in a personal vendetta.

It was the only thing left to break that lead and the chain reaction that had me start again. It was part of a foundation stagnant to that manifestation. It had me relive a drama that forced me to repeat repel and face the corrupt while I got through hell. Warned without fail, a manifested tale.

Towards a destination, devoting myself to a trend that had me repeat an old wound. An expense that had me stagnant beyond validation. A journey that was pointless to that confirmation. For every time I was to reap a reward I would gasp for air. Just to catch a breath of fresh air.

I was given a trace that had me face a case. Every thought wave, had a final, every trace had a case, I had to close. Where I was given the impression, that the royalty to that loyalty, card became part of an impatient game. It had me gamble, an inclination; towards a journey that will save me in the end.

The trace was handing me the royalties that I needed to replace. It was part of a feast, that had me present the corrupt with a final release. I was in debt with a task;

it gave me an intention. I needed to hit back with a violation to that destination. It was part of a threat, that had me reliving that debt.

It served me well at the end of that piece, it took me on a journey that held me to contempt. So, when I caught up, I could catch the corrupt break the cycle. For they had me face another feast, track down those who have intention to undo that review; facing me with caution.

All so I can hit a break, hit back with an invasion to that restoration. For the corrupt had invented a troubled outcome it gave me a chance to hit back in advance. Face another trace and prepare myself for one more vision to that mission. It handed me an extension to that redemption.

For that overview had me face another improvision to that mission. It was giving me the impression I hit a final feast, one where I get in and break the cycle from within. It had me following up on another trend at the end of that feast to help me release and find peace.

It caused an effect and gave me a trace to release that demon at the end of the race. Just so I can catch up and find peace at the end of that lease. For the silence had me hit back with an alliance. It had me repeat restore my energy and rise above and beyond those who knew.

Those who knew had a clue, forced their way in; breaking every rule. Just so they can win, catch up and feed of the energy that created the piece. It was handing me an evolution to replace the old bring forth the new. Release the beast that took me in present me with an extension.

A warrant to that deception, had me face another restitution to that resolution. It led me to believe every faith had me state a fact and follow up on another written acclaim. A division to that restitution become accompanied by a third party. It was part of a redemption that warned me.

I had no infiltration to that conclusion, what I had was a trace. It faced me with an extension to that ending that was pending. It caved in on me and brought me forward straight into an expense that led me towards an extension to that foundation that had me manifesting a journey outdated.

Because every trace had a case and every restitution brought back the end of that resolution. It forced me to predict future event the one where the corrupt took me in fed off me from within and repeated every trace remorsefully facing me with an ending that was pending.

Because they wanted a piece of the action, they had me face another abreaction. It created a trace forced me to get in and feed off the energy that had me face a dead end. It was part of a given, the freedom to disclaim and feed off the trace that had me replace another case.

I had to retreat a trace at the end of the race. It had me feed off the intention. Accomplish another goal so when I reach my peak, repeat catch up and press delete. It handed me a redemption to that manifestation that caused an effect. It gave me trace to catch up and feed off the compilation.

CHAPTER 7

◆ ◆ ◆

WHEN THE SIRENS HIT HEAVEN

It gave me a second chance to restore my energy in advance. I was given a final visit, from those who enter my realm and feed off the trend that served me well. I was left to return for a vendetta; it gave me a second chance to face a trace and repeat an old case.

It brought me forward, breaking the corrupts cycle with a second trial, leading them towards a pathway of denial. Where I was taught a lesson left to release all inhibitions, where every challenge had me refine taste that trace and follow up on another faith that had me feed off the concept.

I had to face a trace trap those who are wrong all along. I was trying to catch up and feed off the concept that had me reserve the edge of reason. It gave me a second chance to return the favour forcing me to hit back with remorse. So, when I reached my pinnacle, the problem will be solved.

Delaying my every move, had me trapping those who condition the mission and feed off the vision. I was served well; it had me cover up another spell. A trace to that case that led me towards a journey of a violation. It led me to a destination, that lined me up for a spurt of energy.

It caused an effect, while creating a trace that served me wisdom; at the end of the race. I was given an implication, that every journey will save me, facing me with an expense and an expose to erase that trace that had confirmed the obvious. Nothing will change unless I catch the culprit.

A trailer of thoughts, had brought me forward. It handed me the faith less likely to invade and the energy that gave me the power to undo and devour. All while I divide and conquer. I had to face a trace entrap another trade and follow up on a brand-new trend in the end.

It took me in and presented me with a curse I could reverse. All I had to do was review revive and follow up on a brand-new dive. It gave me a second chance to hit back with a second coming, Where I stepping into the unknown, faced another trace and repeat at the end of the race.

An evaluation that will present me with a confirmation, that caused an effect. That is when I noticed the trace was unbreakable. I had breached every trace in the end. It was handing me the invasion to restore my energy at every point taken. Leading me towards a journey that cannot be revived.

For every thought had changed, I did not want to be part of that exchange. It had me face another trace. It led the corrupt to an ending that was no longer pending, Presanting me with a lead that will serve me well indeed. It had me accommodate towards a trend stand a fact and force my way in.

I had to push the corrupt off track, just to give in and hand them a failed attempt from within. It had me reverse a curse, face a trace; follow up on a given. So, when I reach my potential, that point of attraction will undo. Feeding off the trace that had me face an abreaction; to that manifestation.

The case opened wide, it gave me a second chance to hit the corrupt in advance. Opening that door that was charming me once more. It gave me thorough investigation, from that evaluation. Harming the corrupt from within, trapping their method in the middle of a session a case with redemption.

It gave me an indication I hit a traditional invasion to that confirmation. It had me face a version of myself, a vision, that will keep me alive. Safe, silent, and deadly; trapping those whom were friendly. Feeding off the trace that had me undo another review; then without notice create a defect.

It had me face another debt; it gave me chance to give in and present the corrupt with a brand-new win. The power to face another trace, had me stagnant to my development. It gave me a chance to override and follow up on a brand-new dive. I was informed of the trace, that served me well.

It had me endeavour to release that beast that forced me to find peace. All while I was given an impression to create a piece that will serve me well at every feast. For I was torn in more than one direction facing the corrupt every time I hit a free ride to the other side.

For I was torn, left to repeat another theme. It had me face a trace and override another theme to that scheme. It put me on a journey that will serve me well, it presented me with an upcoming spell. It had lined me up for a confession to that deception; that forced me off the edge of a revelation.

It had me breaking the silence whenever they saw me fit. It left me to divide conquer and override another sponsor. All while I reach the end of that trend, that served me well at the end of that final spell. It formed an alliance at the end of that verse; it forced me to reveal a nasty thought.

A trace to that case that had me face what I thought was the last resort. It tested my patience and formed an alliance where every thread of redemption will cause an effect. It had me break the system at the end of that trace that had me face another case.

It was causing an effect troubling the corrupt at every trend. For I was left to repeat and restore my energy once more. For I was left to give in face another win creates a war in my piece start fresh and release. I went for a trend created a win then went for a new beginning.

A face that will trace that trap and follow up on another impact. For I took it all in faced another win from within. It had me on the edge of facing a brand-new pledge. It forced me to review and follow up on another exchange, just so I can get in and tackle that entrance from within.

It took me on a journey that served me well from within. Where the corrupt will lose and I will break the silence by trapping those who sweetened the deal and faced me at every spill. It lined me up with a follow up on a brand-new review. It had me facing a trap at the end of that wrap.

It will bring forth a final feast at the end of that piece. It had me face a trace where I was given permission to undo my intuition. It me served me an allegation at the end of that exhibition. It was harming those who were open to discussion. An investigation had opened freely.

Where every time I was handed a line up, the energy serving me well was a lie. It forced me to return and face the corrupt with an investigation to line me up. It had me reach a hold up, cause an effect, face a proposition to that improper theme. The one that had me face a scheme in between.

For that mission led me to revive, hit back with a

step forward. It had Led me towards a direction that will hand me a resurrection to face another deception. A motivation to hand me a foundation to repeat and rebel against the corrupts final evaluation. For every presentation had me naïve.

I was motivated by the distinction to that evaluation; it had me face another trace. It was forcing me to give in and feed off the energy that had me terribly wrong from within. It was part of expenditure that took me on a journey that had me rise above and beyond scrutiny.

It gave me a chance to repeat rebel and follow up on another spell. It saw me as an easy target to release that beast that forced me to undo another forthcoming review. There was always a final validation to confront the corrupt with a foundation; that will lead me to the next destination.

For every trace had me torn in directions that saw me easy. Where every time I was forced to release that feast, I was given a chance to undo that review. Forcing me to disclaim another division to a game that had me face another traumatic effect; at the end of the race.

Where I had no time than the present to repeat and rebel against a momentum; that pushed me off the edge. It forced me straight into a ditch, a dead end, and a follow up. Facing a conspiracy in the end. Where that cause, and effect served me well when I was trapped in the middle of hell.

It had me face a space that had me reverse that nerve. I had to sharpen my sword, create a warning to state a new fact. So, when I reach my pinnacle, I could surely foresee a future event, evidently face a dead end. Then when the time come get back on track without fail.

There was no temptation just a trace that will hand me a brand-new evaluation. It was to restore a past pressure that had me face another test without pleasure. I had to feed off the delay that had me hit a dilemma. For that will of testament was a challenge and a cheap shot to meet my quota.

It had me face another trace causing an effect that pushed me in the corner. It was presenting me with a debt that had me face another threat. I had to restore my energy and feed off the trace that had me foreclose another case. A trap that helped me come first.

All while I feed off the energy that had me face a trace. I had to condition that mission to create an opposition to that case that forced me to erase. All while I curse giving me the power to come first. Trapping the corrupt with a motive handing me the trend to break the silence and start again.

For every competition handed me an evaluation to that denomination. I was taught a lesson and left to break the cycle at every arrival. It was part of a trivial affair that ended in a trivial pursuit. Every trend, ended in tragedy it became obvious I was a parting way with those who had survived a dive.

I had to define that manifestation so when I reached my pinnacle, I can return the favour and start again. Where at the end of that revelation, it will force me to redo and accomplish another clue. I had to acclaim another final review. I had to release, find peace face another trace then release.

So, when the time come, overcome another outcome. It had me conclude to that feast that had me enclose an encounter another trace to that case that took me for a ride and faced me with Genocide. just before I was led to believe that energy that faced me took me in and saved me.

I had to fight back face another trace just to claim another diversion. Because the trace was based on a mission that served me well at every disposal. So that proposal that served me well, hit that forthcoming spell. I had to release that demon that forced me to reclaim another meeting.

I was taught a lesson entertained by the notion to the game. It had me repeating every trace at the end of that case; troubling me with a feast. Presanting me with a kind heart. Forcing the corrupt to break the silence. A forethought was the last resort; it was part of a renewal to that manifestation.

Before it got worse, I had to face another curse. Where every momentum created a piece. It had me face a trial an error and a final vendetta. It had me stepping into a warning that forced me to release that feast. Faced me at the end of that lease. Where the end of that expenditure; delayed me.

It was creating a pointless affair that stirred the pot and faced me; when I hit a flare in the air. A trace, giving to me with an impression I faced them too early. It was hitting the corrupt from within handing me the impression I was about to hit a final review.

A challenge that served me well and brought me forward while I went through hell. I was ignored envied by those who saw me easy. That is when I knew I hit a hold up and an at the expense at the corrupts debt a trace that had me face a trend in the end. An individual aspect that turned sour.

For he who knew was heaving and left me hanging in there. Trying to release that beast that had me facing an encore to that trial that error it created final dilemma. It had me delete delay and press a precious stone in the middle of that contamination that led me to the wrong destination.

Face that trend, with the intent; will meet my standard. An impression that the trace was paused. It was part of a case that served me well at the end of that spell. I was parting ways letting it go so I can continue to grow. For that trend had me break the silence.

It took me in, stalled and faced me with a challenge that had me step into the unknown. For every trace was handing me an evaluation. Before I could cash in and present the corrupt with another vendetta. Pushed in the corner, where my patience ran thin and my loyalty rejected.

My patience tested the trace resurrected, all while I devour, divide and conquer. Following up on a feast, a trial an error and fixation that handed me a resolution to that revolution, I had to try my best to cover up another conquest. It had me reach my potential with appeal.

I was on the brink ready to face another flinch all while I caught up and fed off the present glitch. An action that handed an abreaction from a foundation that had me warned I had no freedom no foundation just a lead to the next destination. I had to face another redemption to that reception.

It forced me to hit an ending that was pending. All while I got back on track and trapped that tactful event. I was led on left to face another trace. Where I was in the middle trying to feed off the riddle. It took me in and faced me from within, all so I can present the corrupt with a key.

It was a challenge to repeat repel, face what I thought was part of an ongoing spell. I was left to return and face a trace, then when the time come overcome another outcome. A trend that put me through it all. It had me face a flaw, a fall from a wall that collapsed; leaving me stating the facts.

It was part of a trend that served me well in the end. Where every trace had me forsake a fake and false case. It was causing an effect, it had me follow up on a trend, a trace that will save me when I hit a dead end. So, when I reach my pinnacle, I could redo that clue; facing another review.

For the left overs were part of a trade, it had me on the edge trapped in the middle of a final pledge. It caused an effect had me face a death threat. So, when I reach my pinnacle, I can remain silent regain points, and hit the corrupt back feeding off the impact that served me at the end of the race.

It forced me to reveal the truth, and hand me a chance to invade in the corrupts privacy. It was hitting them with an entrance that had me step into the unknown. A trace that served me well and brought me through hell. For what they knew and what was supposed happen was personal.

It ended in good faith, for the trace was based on a case and redo another review. It had me follow up on a trend, creating a trace will release that beast. It had me regain a train of thought; it brought me back to what I thought was the last resort. It had me refrain and refine a brand-new game.

I was taught a lesson, left to repeat. It had me on the other end about to repent. It was part of an ending that was pending and a foundation that was never ending. Because everything went belly up, it gave me a second chance to belt the corrupt in advance. I lost my way, trying to get back on track.

Because I was Warned of the outcome, I knew the trace will erase and the only thing remaining was the last thing standing. It was part of an impact that threw me off track. They were trying to press replay and I on the other end fighting for my life ready and willing to break the silence; God-willing.

I had no faith for I knew the corrupt were torn ready

to erupt. No entitlement, just a freeride to embrace the case. It had me pending and the ending was suggesting a truce. I had the energy to create the piece no foundation to eradicate to the next destination.

For that reification was handing me the knowledge and the drama to that case was pending. I was stagnant to my development because every journey had a rate and I could not define that energy because I was hit with a vendetta a constant reminder the drama trapped me in.

The dream became a false reality in-between. I could not fight back; my method became a threat. It presented me with a curse that had me follow up on a view. A return to that theme, belted me in-between. It was a start of a fight, reliable undeniable return; releasing that demon in advance.

Leaving the corrupt dead no more threat at the end of that trend. It had me facing an extension to that redemption. For hell had me restore my energy feeding off the corrupt every time I was handed a challenge to enhance and exchange that good deed; where in the end I did not accept defeat.

It was a bribe to cover up a trace that had me face another. It was part of an extension that branded me when I hit redemption. I was given a chance to hit back in advance, so when I hit the end of that trend the only thing missing was the curse that hit me at the end of that verse.

In the end that dead end, forced me to pretend. It had covered up the last resort it had me return for one more key an everlasting trend that served me well in the end. It was part of a trace extending the case. A release to help me find peace, at the end of that theme; no trap in between.

CHAPTER 8

◆ ◆ ◆

NO LEAD WHEN THE CORRUPT ARE ABOUT TO SUCCEED

When the corrupt catchup, they state a fact, and then cave in on the concept. Assuming their method will overlap that trace. It had me overpower another case, giving me the impression I hit a deception to that wheel of fortune. The one that had me convey another bad day.

There was an overdrive, drafted, in a pathway that had not lasted. It was part of a dream that turned into a nightmare in-between. I was given a challenge that had me refined, it gave me a second chance to delve into a drama that served me well in that ongoing spell.

I was taken by surprise; it had me face another trace. Where the concept had me on the edge trapped in the middle of that pledge. Where I get in and win another tremor; from within. I was taken for a ride it overlooks another stage to the trend; that had me face another dead end.

It took me in at face value, and faced me with an overlap of information. It was part of a challenge that will transform me intellectually. It had me trapped, it gave me with an informal interrogation to the next destination. I had to form an investigation, and trap those who created an expense.

It had me face another trace in the end. I was left to embrace that debut, and face my fear. Follow up on a review, face another trace then take a moment to indulge in what I thought was the last resort. It had me condition the mission give in at every exposure; troubling the corrupt.

For when I was handed that key, I was not grounded I had way too many hangups. Too much drama to overcome, it gave me a chance to interact with those who correct me if I am wrong. A challenge that served me well it gave me a foundation to follow up on the next destination.

I had to overcome, what I thought was a given. It gave me the power to get rid of the forbidden. In the end I had to face another wrong. It gave me a second chance to delve into a trance. It served me well at the end of that race. It had me forthcoming and the event undo; that final review.

It had me face an ending that was pending. The trend that was part of that break, it was part of a warning that had me on the edge. I was about to scheme for another theme. It led me overtake another final review, causing an effect and breaking the silence right through.

I had to feed off the trace, that served me well. It was a given, where the corrupt had me face another vision to that interpretation. I had followed up on an old wound let it all go and set it all free. All so I can continue on my journey and face another tradition; at the end of that mission.

I had to follow up on a dream feed off the drama in-between. I had to encourage the old start new and break the system right through. I lost my faith because those who knew wanted to return and break me siren it had me facing another trace and feeding off the case that caused an effect.

It was handing me the power to overcome and devour a trend that ended in a trace that was pending at the end of the race. It handed me the conclusion to get through, meanwhile trap the corrupt so I can overcome another outcome. Because the method was not prewritten.

It had me overtake and follow up on a traditional affair. An overflow of information caused an effect and created a flare in the air. It brought me forward, leading me to a destination that served me well. It handed me a trace that saved me at the end of the race.

I was taught a lesson and faced with a degree of anxiety because of it. I was off trying to catch a break. Feeding off the energy that had me face a trace. It served me well led me through hell waiting for the right moment to enter that realm. It served me a challenge and put me through hell.

I was trapped, left to override a bribe; enough to survive and then subdivide. It had me creating a challenge that will lead me towards an expense that had me face another burn. It had me return and prepare myself for a trace reaping a reward and claiming what I thought was the last resort.

It did not face me well, for the time it took for me override a trace. Had me pack up and follow up on another case. It gave me a second chance to embrace a case, kick a fuss, and follow up on another rumour. A challenge that had me on the edge, trapped in the middle of a lost cause.

It had me release that beast, accompanied by a championship. It led me on me on create a test to save the beast. Leading me to a destination that forced me off the edge straight into a challenge that will help overcome another outcome. I was given a chance to click collect; overlap another trap.

I had to face another trace; it had me on the edge. It was part of a given pledge. I had to release that beast that forced me to compete compel and put me through hell. It was part of a challenge that had me embrace another case. It put me in a position that had me raise awareness.

I had to feed off the destination, that will remain silent; handing me an evaluation. It tore me the bits, an ending result endeared with feast. The drama was about to unfold; it had me quick, think ready; just to override that drive. I was to subside feed off the trend that had me face a dead end.

Purely to throw me off track, it gave me a chance to enter that realm and face another remedy at the end of that final stigma that served me well. It was part of a trace a given reason to replace that treason. For where it began and for what it was worth; I did not release that feast.

It gave me the energy I needed to find peace. I was on the move, trying my luck on an intention to feed off the corrupt. I was to be released on good faith, but they had other goals. Locking me in treating me like a second-class citizen. Question my self-worth; it had me face a reality in the end.

A challenge I could embrace, had me forced to invade in what I thought was last resort. For the curse was to be reversed and the ending served well. All so I can take a chance in developing another shift to that trace. I was forced to step back take a moment to absorb and feed off the case.

I was led on, charged a fee, had to rely on me to get by. For every trace served me wrong, every method kept me strong. There was glitch, a challenge in the matrix, a follow up on a trick, where the corrupt were trapped getting over the overlap; no connection just a follow up to a deception.

It had me on the edge raising awareness; an awakening on the other side. Waiting for me to override what I thought was the last resort. I had written a wrong, creating a feast, facing another trend at the end of that dead end. Reminding my soul the only thing that could change was the last thing.

It that had me face another train of thought; it held me back an gave me a second chance to get back on track. It was the last thing that brought me forward. Where the edge of reason forced me to repeat replace and face another case. It had me trapping the corrupt in the corner.

It was part of a pointless affair, that had me face another bad omen. It had me trace another trend point the finger towards those who knew and those who had a clue. I was heading towards a fall a trace that had me trapped ready to rise above it all. I was heading towards the wrong direction.

When the time come, overcome an outcome. For every trace, had me face a reselection, to that redemption. I had to return follow up on a feast, catch a few waves then peak. So, when the time was right break that trend that had me fast forward in the end.

I had to embrace another trace get in and feed of the trend that had me forced to pretend. I had to bring forth a lead to give the corrupt another to breathe. A faith less likely to eradicate, for every dream had caused a drama.

Where every lead forced me to breathe.

It led me to believe that the only thing, holding me up was the last thing that saved the corrupt. It was part of a task; that had me face another trace. A challenge I could relate to, it was part of a task that had me face a first and last. Just so I can get back on track and fast forward to that next empath.

It had me face another case, causing an effect that had me return for another yearning. Where every trace tricked me into believing that the case was deceiving. I was given a momentum, that led me towards a presentation that was part of a trial an error; a familiar terror.

There becomes a time, that the rift from that drift, will undo; handing me a clue. Where the end result had me break the system. I had to give in feed off the trial and the error. It had me face a dead end. There was no wrong, nor wright just an everlasting fight; to give me a chance to override a dive.

It was part of a failed attempt, added with another side effect that troubled me in the end. Because The universe had a plan, the trace was rearranged and I on the other end starting again. Where the only thing left was, I grieving over what I thought was last resort.

A given chance to overcome another outcome. There was test that had me fail, and instead of preventing me to give in it gave me another chance to win another inning. I had to follow up and face another conspiracy just to catch up get back and feed off the corrupt.

I had to prevail, then prevent the corrupt from hitting the holy grail. There were several on my raider feeding of the trend. No one was truly helping me; in fact, they played it purely to revive another dive. It had me facing a key that had me return for another yearning.

It had given me the endangerment; I needed to embrace. Then when I gave in follow up on another trace. It had me breaking the silence restarting a new trend. Just so I can catch up and face a new improved journey in the end. I give in, face that case as I embrace a trace.

Hounding the corrupt and breaking the silence at the end was praising me. I hit a dead end of that bend; it had me face another test encouraging me to progress. It forced me to rebuild and start again. That is when I knew the corrupt were on my raider trying their luck to hand me bad luck.

There was a bad energy, an omen attached to my spirit. It forced me to repeat and regain consciousness all while I was let down and hit with a final countdown. It was lingering around the point of no return. It had me face another day giving me the impression I hit denied reaction.

The air was misty its smelt musky, and that is when I knew I hit a break through. The room with a view became a separate entity, it had me release that beast. It gave me a second chance to catch up and keep up with the program. It finalised that trend that served me well in the end.

It forced me to repeat and face a trace. Then without

wanting to, gave me a chance to release that beast. I had forced my way in and create a new improved journey from within. The warning remained the same it gave me a second chance to terrorise the corrupt all the way.

It had me conditioning the mission, releasing all inhibitions. I had lay the law rely on the corrupt to get by so when I reached my peak the ending would be pending and the trace would expend long enough for me to return and break that chain that had me face a case at the end of the race.

Leaving the corrupt dead to the bone, had me on the edge; rising above and beyond. It gave me a chance to survive another trace at the end of that race. It forged it way the through that rough spot. It forced me to replace another given momentum; to a game that was gambling my dream away.

It gave me a release to that feast, handing me the end of what I thought was a dead end. I had to challenge the remaining goal, create a trace, and finalise a test. Where every piece had me release the beast. Creating a warning that will serve me well; trapping me when I passed that casting spell.

It had me creating an anomaly where every thought brought back a memory. All while I catch up and finalise that trend that saved me well in the end. I had to acclaim another division to the game that diverted when I hit the end of that trend. It had me on the edge leading the pact.

Then when I least expect it feed off, he who knew. Then

reap my reward and break the spirit of he who had a clue. I caved in on the concept holding he who knew hostage as I continue on my method. Then face that tremor with a trial and error. All while I feed off, he who knew.

For it was he who knew wanted to break me, all by leading others to shame me. He assumed he could hire he who had a clue, forcing him to face with adrenalin; action that handed me abreaction. Where the system chased me and left me warned of what was to come from that outcome.

All while I break the silence, it had me hitting back with an alliance; creating a war in my peace. All so he can be prepared for a new improved scare. It had me replace a challenge, a trace, a final internal affair. Feeding off the trend, all so I can return the favour and face a hint; at the end of that race.

A given reason to burn every page, brought me forward, creating a war in my domain. For those whom were rewarded, had me stagnant to my development. There was a suggestion, that had me to close for comfort, waiting patiently for the moment to repeat rebel; causing an effect.

It had me deleting a defect, an emotion, that had me admiring the irony. Testing the patience of he who knew, trapped me in the corner about to face another trauma. The energy that stated the fact forced me in and had me interact with the devil I knew the demon within.

Where the evil spirit who took over my energy to feed off me from within. It had me faced with a reality that lined me up with an expense that left me warned I was nowhere near that serenity that brought me back to reality. It served me a sight that gave me the impression I hit the end.

The deception that saved me then, forced me to repeat delete then take the initiative and face me with another trace at the end of the race. It reserved me the right to follow up with a condition now. It gave me a second chance to force my way through on a dream that faced me in-between.

I had to face another reality; all while I belt the corrupt in between. I was hit right before I hit a competition. It was part of a trace that was pending and I was left with no defence. No back up, no release to that feast; not even a given reason, to hit back with treason.

I hit a trap that took me in and fed off me from within. It left me prejudice, pointing the finger at he who had no energy to create the piece. It forced me to return face a trend, that was never ending; only pending. That is when I knew that every follow up had me on review.

I was on the move living in my own domain trapped within the same old game. For those who knew had me face another trace, it was giving me the impression I fell into a refreshing development. It had me cause an effect creating a piece and feed off the feast.

For those who knew were was too close. They were creating a war in my peace, just so they can find a way out. Hitting me with a trace that had me fast-forward to the next. I was given a reason to trace that trap that had me on the edge of redeeming another trend in the end.

I had to cause an effect, trap those who descend. Just to get a glimpse of a future gamble. I was taught a lesson left to reprieve forced to return repeat and follow up on another deed. I had to uncover another cover up. I had to trace that case that had me on the edge.

Served well, with a given chance to put the corrupt through hell. An expense, that was put to the test parted. For what went wrong, had me face ahead what I thought will be the last resort. It put me in a position that served me a terrible proposition. A redemption with no contamination.

Just an evil sense of retaliation, from an old wound. It had me condition a proposal, with an expense that served me well in the end. It was part of a trace that had me embark for an extension to that redemption that had me forced to acclaim another violation to that manifestation.

In the end I felt the trace became a worrisome affair. It was accompanied by a challenge that had me turned, facing another trend. Warning me I hit a dead-end. Because I was taught a lesson, it trapped those who pretend. Where every competition handed me an imposition to that evaluation.

It had me stirring the pot and forcing me to release that demon that led me towards another vision. It had restored my energy handing me a condition to claim my clarity. It was part of a mission to release all inhibitions. Reporting those whom were habitual to that opposition.

CHAPTER 9

◆◆◆

THE EDGE OF REASON HANDED ME TREASON

I had to cancel the old, start new and feed off that stagnation that served me a recognition. I was left to remain indecisive to a game that was prize winning. It lined me up for a feast that served me well at the end of that spell. It had me cave in on the concept to that manifestation.

Waiting for the wrong move had come to be, I was given a reason to break the system and face another trace. All so I can catch up and feed off the conspiracy. It took me on a journey leading the pact. An added confusion to that conclusion, handed me the result I needed to acclaim a division.

It broke every momentum, that served me a proposition. For I was left to return, release the beast follow up on a turn of events and trace that trend that had me start again. that was meant to face me with a conclusion. The thought that come my way had me facing another bad day.

It restored my energy took me on a path then in the end faced me when the dark saw me easy. The thought caved in on the trace that had me face another case. It took me on a path that had me returning for one more yearning. It caused an effect took me on a trend detecting a dead end.

I had to delve into a development, that took me in and faced me with a challenge from within. It had me in admin folding up and feeding off the trace that served me well. For that forthcoming reason, it had me requesting an evaluation. All while questioning my truth; an assessment to break the cycle.

It had me sitting on a precious perch, leading the pact on many facts. Where the tradition had me face another vision and a version of myself that I was not aware of. A trace that had me face the end and beginning of an end. A journey where the energy that stated the facts got me back on track.

It had me feeding off the energy at force. It was part of a given; to hand me remorse. It had me fail a feast, pass a test, then continue on my journey with progress. A vision to that competition served its purpose. An evaluation every time, I had a game to gamble; a scheme to part with that theme.

I had to process then digress for the first and last decision was not part of the competition. I could not look forward nor face another waring, for the corrupt had me on the go giving in. Trying their luck to undo undergo another show. It was my way of getting the job done and moving forward.

The trace had me on the run failing the corrupts outcome. I had to progress that contest take it with a stride then when the time come overcome the outcome. When I reach my peak, I could embrace that trace that served me well, it had me focused. It put me on a journey; from heaven back to hell.

It was to hand me a key that will give me the facts to state. Handing the corrupt a dead end at the end of that trend. Even though it was haunting me at the end of that cause of action. I knew I hit a hold up because the corrupt had set me up for a fall so I never get up.

For those who knew, created a piece. It was leading me towards a journey that had me remain at peace. I had to remain the same cleanse my spirit and not allow the naysayers to get in my way. Emotionally drained from a game that was tormenting me and leaving me revived.

When I reached my peak, I could remain sturdy and alive. Create a test that will push the corrupt in the corner so I can progress. I needed to process, before I fell into another test. I was to face a trace and repeat after the fact. So, when I reached my peak, I could get back on track and press delete.

It had me facing another case, it was feeding off the remedy; a legal document. It had me breaking the extremity forcing me to replace and overcome another outcome. It was part of a trend that had me forced to hit back and pretend. All while the corrupt took me in and fed off me from within

It was part of a lead, that had me face another good deed. Where every trace hit every case handed me a trauma that served me well heaving at me and the outcome in the outskirt forcing me to return and reclaim another division to game that had me stall once again.

An outcome I needed to get through, had me on the move. I was caving on the concept, catching up on a final hit. It was causing an effect and belting the corrupt with an entrance to that trace that had me replacing another case. It had me on the edge served well; presented with an upcoming spell.

I had to return, to that theme that had me face a scheme in-between. A losing battle, that had me embracing the truth. For every challenge I faced had me face another trace. It was creating a war so I never face a losing battle. Every trace had me on the edge presented with a brand-new pledge.

It led me towards a condition. that had me face a proposition. It served me well at the end of that competition. It kept me balancing on one knee, trying my luck not to lose fail, nor fall into a bad sail. I was returning to break the spirit, of he who intentionally went out of his mind; to break mine.

Because those who knew wanted to face me, with no war in mind only the battle because the war was not over it just begun it handed me an outcome that served me well in the long run. They wanted me to give in after the win. An unfair battle where they hit me with a conspiracy and run.

I could not stand to fail a challenge; by ignoring the signs. So, I decided to give in on the gratitude; I could return confirm the obvious. While I create the piece, forced to look within and find peace. While I trace another debt, that served me well and forced me to get in and feed off the win.

It was part of another win, getting me to release that piece that faced me from within. It was an ending that was pending that had me surrender at every contamination, returning the favour forced me to reveal. Warned I hit the end of that trend that stood clear and faced me with a dead-end.

It had me curse that verse, face another feast. It had me break the silence and prepare me for what I thought was part of the last resort. For that piece was a condition that put me on a mission to break free from that proposition. Where The energy that stated the facts had me face a nasty trace.

It pushed me off track, straight into a final, an inning that handed me denial. I went back and forth lending a hand to he who took me in. It forced me to feed off the energy so he can follow me from within. Leaving me suffering, while the rest went hunting; a reason for me, to hit back with treason.

I was on the move trapped in the middle of a safe environment. Rest assured, every game will hand me a safe haven. It gave me a chance to hit back in advance, trying my luck to face another case. Offering the corrupt a final challenge. It will hand them denial and I a free ride to the other side.

It had me cause an effect, and feed off the defect. There was an expression of interest, an invasion to that tradition that gave me a final embrace. Before I was hit with a brand-new case every follow up and every faith had me forced to hit back with remorse.

For every challenge had its vision and every curse had its admission. I was admired from afar, by those who knew and could not wait to screw me right through. I was given the opportunity to rise above the scrutiny. The trace had me wonder, what come over me and handed me such a blunder.

I was given a trace, that led me to believe no trend was not strong enough to break my cycle because I was forced to hit back with remorse facing another cause. It was handing me the invasion that destination that took me in. It restored my energy from within.

An energy that forced me to reprieve, prepared me for a good deed. It also gave me the power to upstage and undo that knot that had me face an extension to that redemption. In the end of that trace, I was left to embrace a trend. Then when the time come overcome another outcome.

Because I was out numbered it broke me as such. It taught me a hell of a lesson, one lived and the other learnt, where get in win and repeat that trace that served me well from within. In the end all I could do was upstage those who knew and make sure those who had a clue never get through.

Warning me every thread had me cause an effect. It was leading me to a destination that handed me the right to hit with force. Then get back on track and face another consolation to that destination. A trace at the end of race had me forced to reveal what I thought was a steal.

It had me cut then hit me with a trend that served me well in the end. Where that thread rot there was no longer a strength to that string of events. I was faced with a case that left it to the imagination. I had to remember a past event, so when the trend becomes overbearing the trial cut.

It ended, in tragedy where I was given a chance in advance to break the cycle. I was left to feed of the drama that had me release that beast. I had to encourage my spirit to restore my energy. So, when I reach the end of that trend, the only thing left was the last thing on my mind.

I was to break the cycle and decline everything. For the corrupt were expected to challenge me in a way where I got in and played the game too. But all it did was release all inhibitions. Then when I least expect it repeat report and rebel against those who put me through hell.

It undid and had me face another trace at the end of that review. The energy to that method handed me a terrible act of kindness. It surrounded me with a clue, that will bring me hope and the power to return and devour. So, when I reach my pinnacle, the only thing standing was the everlasting theme.

A scheme that forced me to hit back and break the cycle in-between. I was entering unknown territory, a case that caused an effect. It was to give in and feed off the trace that had me forced to hit back with remorse. The drama was left to the imagination, where every trend had me a clueless.

It forced me to revive another technique, where this time around I case close it all and leave the corrupt falling into a trace that had me embrace another case. I had to catch up and feed off the corrupt so I can get through. Warning me there was no given; just a competition to break the cycle.

I had to feed off the admission, face another competition. Warning me, the energy I had, was nowhere near the energy that phased me. So, when the end of that tragedy took its toll, I could unfurl divide and conquer and step into a story untold. The one that gave me the power to unfold.

I was given a reason to hit back with treason. A follow up to the next destination, where I had to compromise what I knew. As I fed off the competition, to reach the next vision my temptation to hit back diminished. I had no gain to fall back on, because the corrupt had reached their limit.

What I knew and what I was given handed me a genius idea. I was to stir the pot give he who knew a challenge so I can skip that too. For the corrupt had a chance to repeat, but I was not in it to create the piece. I was in it to bring war into peace. It forced them off the edge straight into a dead end.

It had me watching them from another angle while they rot in silence; all while I reach my pinnacle. Then when the time come overcome another outcome. It had me feeding off the trace that had me facing another case where every ordeal forced me to reveal what I thought was the last resort.

I had to push the corrupt in the corner, face another warning. It had me on the edge of reason, warning me again there was no foundation; to mark another destination. Without failing another mission, I had to cancel it all force my way in and present the corrupt with another win.

Then without further a due, incur another avenue. Where every feast trapped me in the corner and released the beast. It created anomaly in the corrupts vision pausing an effect; so, they never win a competition. Where the only thing left was for me to give in and feed off the trace from within.

I had to face another case, catch up, and break the cycle from within. It took me down a pathway, feeding off drama that straightened me out. It was part of a devotion that handed me a promotion. I had no case to erase, and a challenge to overcome another outcome.

For what I had was an informant who watched from another angle. Deserting those who endeavour to devour. Caused an effect and handed me an evolution to break the system and feed off the trend that served me well in the end. I tried my luck attempting to face a trace; feeding off the bad luck.

I had to follow up to another vision, complete that composition. Then entertain myself with a trace that handed me the empowerment I needed to embrace. All while I compare that energy to a dramatic effect; the one that handed me the entrance I needed to resurrect.

Where the corrupt wanted to succeed; leaving me behind an energy that had me rise. I was given a reason to overcome a treason. For those who knew took me in and faced me with a trauma that lined me up with a test that had me release. For that interaction with the at physic was intrinsic.

It taught me a lesson; handing me a brand-new aroma. Where I was on the move, terrorised by the trauma that took me by surprise. It handed me a validation to accompany me to the next final destination. For those who were forced to hit back with remorse; were encouraged.

It was part of a fight that turned to my favour. It developed into a trace, that had me stand clear. I was not aware of the impact. It served me well and presented me with an entrance to put me in a position worse than I can imagine. I went through hell trying to make sense of my reality.

It led me towards a passageway, that had no meaning to me. I was put on a journey that had me cause the effects. Handing the corrupt a chance to resurrect. I had to trace that case, embrace that trend feed off the impact and start again. I had to embrace the end; the beginning of a dead end.

It was part of a new thought one that had been part of a terrible lie. I was on the move trapping me at every final. I hit the last resort and the only way I could validate that trait was pressure the corrupt and face another entrance to that endeavour; that had me face another interrogation.

I hit the next destination validating what I thought was the beginning of a new improved inning. I was on the edge, creating a new pledge. Warning me, the end of that trace, will only come to fruition when I hit the corrupt at an intersection. I hit a limit, trapped in the middle of a rough spot.

A point of no return, had come and given me a kick start. Not only the corrupt were caught out but they hit doubt. I was given a chance to hit back in advance, pushing the corrupt in the corner. I was facing an interrogation, opening an enquiry; creating a test that had me fast-forward to the next.

All because every turn of events was based on a case that had me fast-forward to the next review a challenge that got me through. Where every thought took me in and fed off me from within. Because I was needed to release those fears; it had me survive on a journey that lied.

I was not given an opportunity to prove my innocence. I was stuck in the middle fighting of a lost cause. Where every thought that come my way; part of the last resort. It was to have me reach my peak as I rose above that feat. A trend that served me well in the end of that travesty.

It was basically part of a trace, forced to hit back with an alliance. But I was on my own I had no freedom nor did I have the back up. What I had was the end of one journey and the beginning of a new yearning. A challenge that served me well and brought me forward all while I went through hell.

A thought that took me in and faced me from within. It was forcing me to break the energy that saw me as an easy target. Several were in the background trying their luck facing me with bad luck. Stabbing me in the back while they reap a reward and attempt to fail another sale.

I was on the edge, trapped in the middle of a case that casted a spell that wrapped me up. It was causing an effect, that took me on a journey that had me resurrect. It had been hunting me down looking for reasons to face me and follow a route to sabotage my journey.

It was trapping those who knew and those who had a clue. Driven from a past event, that broke the silence and had me pay off another debt. An affair that became pointless, took me in, and faced me with a trace that served me well. It forced me to undo and follow up on another review.

The drama had no praise to abide by; the rules had changed. I was given the chance to face a proposal. Wanting to get recognition, for that mission; releasing all inhibitions. I was to return and restore my memory, that had me face a trace. An endangered task that fed off the impact.

CHAPTER 10

◆ ◆ ◆

FACING REALITY, WITH A KICK START IN MOTION

I became an emotional wreck; my anxiety kicked in feeding off me from within. That is when I knew I was lied too; my instincts were invasive. It confirmed, someone was intruding in my affairs trying to claim another division to the game. It was part of a trace that handed me power to erase.

For the power to acclaim that trend had me face a dead end. It was to cancel out the corrupts method a motive that will give me the chance to belt the corrupt in advance. I had to claim another award to that trace that had me hold on to another case.

I was left to release that beast, then face another feast. All while I catch up and feed off the corrupt. It had me on the edge of creating a deception to the corrupts final manifestation. Handing me the energy I needed to repeat; get through and press delete.

I could not figure out why I was left to produce another key. When all was done and I all I had to do was create a follow up to that outcome. For that free ride that had me stepping into a trend that served me well. For that final review had me face an entrance; handing the corrupt a dead end.

I was lined up forced to hit back face another trace. Then when I least expect it, trap those who took me in and attempted to feed off me from within face another energy while I catch up and accompany it with a final vendetta a challenge that will force me to hit back with a tremor.

For that trend that led me to believe I had no freedom to pretend. Handed me an invasion to that destination that caused an effect. I was being discriminated against, led to believe the energy that forced me to compete had me convey and trap those who press replay.

It led me towards a journey, that served me well. It presented me with a forthcoming spell. A defect, that gave me a second chance to delve into a proposal. Forced me to revive another survival technique to stay alive. For the finals became real and I fell into a third wheel.

All I knew I was being stalked held back pushed in the corner and left to suffer. All so the corrupt prosper. It became part of a forceful event, where every trace had me on the mend. It had me testing the edge creating a pledge and facing another trial an error and a brand-new vendetta.

It was part of a fierce event, leaving me stagnant to my development. For what I thought was part of a fragment of my imagination, was a true fact; happening behind my back. So, when I caught up and created a defence to the corrupts fascistic event. It gave me a chance to vent while the rest descend.

I entered the trace a given reason to accomplish another treason. I had to face a trend at the end of that trace. It handed me a dead end a trip down memory lane that will hand them the ordeal to fail them at every deal. So, when I reach my peak, the only thing standing was I reviving a technique.

When I did, it was too late the corrupt returned and hit me with love then hate. It got to the point I was given a challenge that served me wrong. It was feeding off the trace that had torn, giving me the impression I gave in for way too long. I was, unattained with no clarity to speak off.

Handed me a wrong path, I was written off and left to suffer while the rest prosper. Reporting them made no difference, hitting them and running made them release peace. It had them repent, even allowed them to become stronger; while I vent. It had me stepping into unknown territory.

I was not welcome, I was led astray, passing tests and initiating a final request. It had me facing a demon, one who had strength it gave me a trap that had me repent at the end of that threat. It forced me to release that beast that consciously took me in and fed off me from within.

I needed to be safe, feel safe and I needed to know that those who closed me up took me in and fed off me from within will break the cycle and never win. It forced me to hit back with treason. Analysing every component with a challenge, that will hand me an extension to that redemption.

It was part of a cunning momentum to witness. All because I was free, ready, and willing to release that beast that had me face another feast. For it was creating a challenge to bring forth unity. Initiating the truth, creating a cause and effect feeding of the entourage.

It had me return and fast forward to the next trace. It handed me a final restoration to that manifestation that caused an effect. It handed me the energy to help me look beyond what I thought was the last resort. It was part of a trap, that broke the system; so, I can get back off.

It had me finalising that request that was manifesting another trace, at the end of that feast. It forced me to find peace in the most awkward places. Because that case was wide open the wound exposed it attached so many maggots to my spirit. The bad memories became part of that unity.

It left me feeding off the scrutiny the case was forced by the trace the trend was left to hit me with a dead end. It had me replace the old the new and the entitlement that got me through. It caused an effect that conditioned the mission so I never return for the same proposition.

Where the only trace left behind was the trend that had me face a dead end. A competition that was part of the mission became apparent to the opposition. That is when I knew I hit the end of that trend and the suffering will bring back the unity to face me with a trial an error and a final vendetta.

It led the corrupt to a dead end. All while I got in and fed of the trend from within. While the rest prosper, I was left eye witnessing another theft. I hit the unknown, warned of what was to come from that outcome. A foundation that forced me to hit back with remorse.

When the time come overcome an entertainment, a second coming that was forthcoming. I had to hide behind the truth that became a lie. A trace that had me face another case. For the method forced me to reveal a trial and error. It served me the truth, and saved me at the end of that trend.

It had me face another case, cut all ties while I step into the valley. Pray to God, that their mission was part of a vision, based on the corrupts greed. A dream where it will collapse their light will dim and their foundation will become a meltdown; so, I can rise above and beyond the occasion.

I had to come to terms with the fact my journey was being tarnished. For everyone I met taught me a lesson. A valuable one in fact it had me give in and follow up on a new tradition. This time around I was not going to lose another dollar, just to give the corrupt a chance to repeat another trance.

For that reason, I decided to hit back with treason. My method was based on another case. I just kept going on with it, not give in; nor even try to lead the pact or win another inning. What I was trying to achieve had me facing an endeavour. To devout and devour the corrupts final vendetta.

I did not know how many obstacles would come my way. It had me meeting one individual who had it in for me all the way. I was to experience highs the lows the lead was undone and the entrance to the unknown will hand me a case that will send me above and beyond past that used by date.

I had to get through, follow up on a review. Then when the time come forgive and forget let it go and hope for the best. I had come to terms with the fact those who knew were in knots were not friends. They were enemies sabotaging my existence, pretending they cared.

In fact, it was a lie to keep the peace. They were trying their luck to harmonise with what I thought was the last resort. Because I was hit with an excuse, it was part of an unprecedented event an end of that cause that fell into a retainer. It was to bring forth a challenge of no return.

For that reason, I had to face a condition to clear the air. It had me feed off the trace that served me well at the end of that spell. It had me trending, forced to fight back hit with a tremor. It was based on a trial-and-error handing me the evolution to create a challenge that served me well.

For that forthcoming spell, was embracing the end. Handing me the conformation I needed to release that feast. It had me face a beast, entering the unknown with a trace that will hand me a key. Presanting with a foundation that had me face a reserved challenge.

It was giving me the impression every challenge had me forsake a conclusion. It was part of a restitution that had me foreclose another reason. I had to belt the corrupt with treason just to get back on track and break the system. I was served the wisdom I needed to get back on track.

It was part of a reunion, that lined me up for conclusion. It had me back tracking, leading me to a destination that served me well at every reservation. All while the corrupt were facing a challenge forcing their way in. They were facing another competition, that served me well from within.

I was presented with an energy that was fermented. It served its purpose that saved me at every challenge. It gave me the energy I needed to raid those whom were conceded. I was to feed off the trend, that served me well in the end. Where I hit a trace, that handed me an emblem.

I was to embrace what I thought will encourage the corrupt to speak the truth. For those who knew and those who had a clue had me face another challenge. It gave me the impression the journey was no longer stagnant it was part of an event that had me facing another warning in the end.

It was hitting me with a clue at the end of the race. It gave me a second chance to delve into a trance. I hit a trial, where corrupt saw me as an easy target. So decided to give within reason. I saw my light taken for granted and my trace forsaken. Where every thought saw me as an easy target.

It forced me to return with one thing on my mind. A final dilemma that had me an amendment, it gave me a chance to trace give in and finalise that reason that put me through treason. For the corrupt dived into a tremor, and forced me to get in and create another dilemma.

I had to repeat my destiny from within to cancel out what I thought would become the last resort. For I was stuck in the middle of a forthcoming riddle. I had to hit back with a conscious awareness. Force my way in and face another trace handing the corrupt an extension to that redemption.

A turn around to that event of past test, had come to my attention. I felt the trace and the drama undo that tension. I had to fight back feed off the impact create a piece and remind myself there was no trouble, nor drama just another trace to redo and replace a review to that clue.

A challenge that had me seek validation; so, I can find peace. Created a catch up, all while I caved in on the concept; breaking the system. It was handing the corrupt a dead end at the end of that trend. A final release on my end; because I found peace. Trying to undo what I thought was the last resort.

It had me forced to feed off the energy that was left behind. It had me questioning what I thought was part of a final revelation to that destination. In fact, it was the beginning of I living in denial. It was handing me the resolution I needed to confront the corrupt.

When the time come, I was to overcome another outcome. It faced me with a vision, that trapped me at every exposure. The end becomes clear a beginning of an expose, part of an energy that served me well. It forced me to repeat put me through hell facing another challenge.

I found opportunity to hit back, with a second trial. An informative challenge that handed me denial. Because I was left to repeat a trend that became invalid and those who knew were about to get a taste of their own filth. It faced me with a choice that hit me periodically in the end.

I was to hit back with a determination to hand the corrupt a final destination. For that manifestation forced me off the edge, straight into a faith, less likely to erase and more likely to accommodate. For the end of that final vendetta had me feeling I hit a win; that pushed the corrupt off the bend.

It gave me second trail to hit the corrupt back with denial. Straight into a final restoration an outcome that will tongue the corrupt at the end of that manifestation. I was trapped in the middle of a collage. A trend that had me leaving them facing a trial an error and final dilemma.

I had to face a trace handing the corrupt denial at the end of the race. the trace had me cancel another violation to that destination it caused an effect and broke the silence so I can resurrect. The case was pending and for that reason it was causing an effect; it had me rely on no one.

I had nothing to lose and all to gain for the corrupt saw me easy. It pushed me off the edge purely to drive me insane. I was given an opportunity to rise above the scrutiny. Where every challenge served me well and handed me an ending that brought me forward straight in to a hell hole.

The cycle broke, so I can resurrect. I was drenched in an emotional drainage; it had me face another fear. Giving me the impression I hit the end of that depression with redemption. I was falsely accused left to delay another damn day just to catch a glimpse of the corrupts finally.

It had me replay a first and last key. It was part of a trace that served me well at the end of that forthcoming spell. It took me in and presented me with a brand-new key. A final interrogation to that manifestation. For that trace took me in and faced me with a case that trapped me from within.

It was based on a scene from the past; it created a piece that took me on a journey that had me release. For the energy that had me foreclose the status was part of a hiatus. It had me face a fear trace a case and follow up on a mission. It taught me a lesson that had me flaunted.

I was haunted by a past proposition, so when I reached my peak, the drama will take its toll. I was to face a trace, that lead the pact, that had fed off the impact; at the end of that trend. I hit a high distinction a level of deception. All while I gave in and prepared my soul for a new role.

For that energy, that fed me well had me on a whim. It created a false and unreliable win. It had me forced to hit the corrupt with an entrance from within. A trace that served me well, and prepared me with a challenge that had me spared. Waiting for the next trauma to come my way.

It had prepared me for an extension to that redemption. It lined me up for one more extension. All while I went through hell looking from within to debate what challenge will bring me forth and what mission will break the competition. Hitting the end of that trend; changed was the agenda.

It was the energy that had me face what I thought was the end of that case. But it was the beginning of an upcoming event. For the opening to a trace that had me foreclose another case. I had to refine another trip down memory lane. It had me trace that energy that formed an alliance.

For it gave me a proposal, at the end of that tradition it had me face another cause an effect. It gave me a second chance to get back on track and break the challenge. I was handed an opposition to create a better momentum. For I was given a chance to step in to a new improved avenue.

I was on my way listing those who hit me and ran, giving me the opportunity to belt them in advance. It forced me to hit back with an advantage that served me well. It saved me at the end of that trend it pushed me in the corner and handed me a dead end.

I was given an expense, that served me well at the end of that upcoming spell. For that reason, I was taught a lesson. It had me reliving a relentless amount of disgust. It left me rising above that deception, and repeating an old wound purely to catch up break.

For the silence that led me to release that beast. A given presentation to hand me a brand-new investigation. It had me feed off the corrupt break the silence pretend I never knew, all while I follow up on a review. I was handed an interpretation, that served me well at every destination.

I was returning for a chance to hit back in advance. When I reached the end of that dead end the rest will follow, I will hit an ending that was pending. I was given a reason to develop a trace so when I hit the end of that tither the emotional blackmail will fall out of place.

Hitting the corrupt at every trace, created a recital from a past event. It handed me a challenge that served me well at the end of that spell. That reaction to break the cycle had me face a trial. It was part of a given a chance for me to start again. It was a given, to receive and break the system.

A silent entrance to the forbidden was revived. A past deception became an operable. I could treat it the way I saw fit. Then when the time come cause an effect trace that defect and create a piece to follow up on another feast. Handing me the invasion, to step into a challenge; that served me well.

The event in total, had me face a trace; a given. It was my way of getting in, taking over, and tracking down those who were stalking me to get through. It had me on the run, assuming each trace handed me a case it caused an effect and create a challenge to get back on track and follow up on a debt.

I was on the move creating a war in the corrupts piece. It had me face another trend at the end of that stagnant affair. It had me start again facing what I thought was a warning. In fact, it was the beginning of an ending, added with a technicality. A pending trace that was never ending.

It had me feeding of the trend, breaking the system, and starting again. By the time I hit the end of that challenge the presentation was pending. A trap that was never ending, was a given part of a trend that had me facing another dead end. A forced energy had me on the edge pretending again.

It gave me a second chance to return the favour in advance. It forced me to review, catch up, and finalise that energy that had me paused an effect. It had me trace a trap give in and feed off the impact. I had to retrieve that second trail and face another entrapment to that case.

All so I can get in, get back on track, and start again. I had to revive a follow up on another dive. It gave me a chance to hit back with reasonable doubt. I had to force my way through, an edge feeding off the trace that had me follow up on a case. Handling the corrupts methodical method; with ease.

All so I can skip that too, it had me hit back with remorse and a challenge to give in so I can catch up and find another grid. A challenge that will hand me the key to the next and final degree. I had to release that beast, follow up on a trace that had me start again.

By the time they hit the end of that trace, the trend was transparent. It was pending and that is when I knew that final review was about to bring forth clarity to those who knew. It was challenging me at the end of that trend. It had me on the bend and never-ending trial.

It became a force to be reckoned with. Giving me the edge of reason to accomplish and acclaim another treason. By the time the corrupt returned to hand me bad luck; I was long gone ready and willing to declare and follow up on anther trace. A given reason to prepare myself for one more case.

A treason that had me follow up to the next hold up. Because I was too busy trying to invade in the privacy of those who endower to devour, it had me face another trace forced to hit back with remorse. It brought me forward straight into a deception that handed me redemption.

I was to give in, trace those who win and follow up on key. Where every trap took over, and handed me an evaluation to the next destination. For that case gave me the imposition where I was taken for a ride an indication, I was way over the top hitting back with dictation.

All while I was uncovering up a presentation; leading me to the next destination. For the corrupt were back on track trying their luck to break the system; following up on another vision. With a composition ready to hit back the exposure had become part of the impact.

I was on the other end, trying my luck to overpower. Hitting the corrupt with a division to that mission. Where I get in divide conquer, feed off the trace that had me fast forward to the next final case. Where one thing led to another, and I was hit; terrorised with redemption.

Amen

To be continued...

ABOUT THE AUTHOR

Panagiota Makaronis

I am not going to boast about myself, my education my family values or views. In the end what can I say life is what it is and everyone has their presentation.

What level of education I have is not important here, the fact that I have lived through death threats, dead ends, and the Demons in my head is enough for me to say! Good reddens, to hard labour.

Life to me has been nothing but expectations with several disappointments, on the hope I get somewhere trusting people when they were meant to help me was another story.

Having said that how many times have I heard people say I am helping you, I let my guard down and it ends up a never-ending Drama a story. Where if I was to repeat will end up worse than the first.

Every goal I set for myself so far though, I have achieved. This book is one of them.

But at what expense I had to endure, just so I do not lose faith in myself and in Humanity along the way. Others who knew could not wait to trace test my patience on the hope they erase my passion and end the race before me.

Because I was living and breathing in a society full of competitors, trying to compete with me and entering my realm on the hope they can harm me for they assumed that had more man power than me.

My theory is just to prove that the world is Governed, not just by everyone you meet but also by the way you witness and see yourself. It plays a huge part when you are about to end one journey and rehearse a new path.

A journey I wish not to return and replay, if anything I just want to move forward not look back and return for revenge. Because my opponent lost a fight and could not harm me so he decided to alarm everyone on the hope they cave in on it start an Allianz and harm me that way.

It left cursing the ones who were reversing and rehearsing, just so they can return stir the pot and leave me stagnant. Stuck in a world of my own sitting in self-pity, no way out unless I fought my way out.

That created more war in my peace because those who knew me, knew me well, fighting back was the only way they can prevent going through hell.

In the end all it did, was make things worse, for they were making mountains out of mole hills. However, the interpretation was enough for me to see I was on the right track the risks I took was based on not losing my faith or myself because others were doubting me and create anomaly.

They were haunted by me and my spirit they could not handle my presence or wait to see where they could hit me and run with a dead-end challenge. The only way out was to hold on to my dream repeat rebel and hit with an All might Spell.

I had come across several individuals who could not wait to break my fighting spirit, constantly on the move of how to kill me and my spirit.

The constant rejection, let down from those stalkers who had nothing better to do then follow me everywhere. Enter my realm just before I am about to make it happen, it got to the point I was failing every test because of it.

Eventually I gave in it was evident, let my Guard down on the hope and the condition there abuse and their method return and back fires.

Having to pick myself up after being pushed straight of the edge from so called Evil! Family friends and Associates, those who I call the corrupt.

What can I say a job is a job well done, level of education is based on life lessons? Everyone has a theory and so do I. Whether you agree is another story to just agree to disagree.

All the studying I did gave me an outlook, a method and outcome where sometimes I look back and wish I never entered but again I would not be here if I didn't.

The theory of here see and speak no evil to me is a lesson lived and lesson learnt. A challenge I can honestly say, it was testing a trace for me to embrace look back and erase. As I face my fears overcome another failure to that feast that handed me release.

As I look ahead and watch my journey unfold with a story untold, it will become a final phase to the next part of my truth. A challenge that will give me the indication I was on my path a feast to release peace.

Everyone is looking for answers and the hope to live

through life with comfort passion and a reason without having to deal with treason.

My memoirs are based on my journey and life lessons, it is all in the book in the end only time will tell, what can I say will be me, keeping up with the programme my way.

Not the way they state it because I hesitate to wonder who is really saving me here. For in the end the matter of facts, is in my hands, because I am an individual. My thoughts are based on my life lessons and no one can challenge or change that.

I know every challenge has its presentation and what I see is I am about to shut one door and open another. Where my vision is no longer impaired and whatever is enlisted to get to this point is no longer in the back burner.

It belongs in my spirit it is mine I earned it! I am just messenger, just passing through the rest remains Ancient History added with a Mystery.

For those who read will understand read between the lines, because my point of view is a venture to next quest on hope I can make a difference to humanity for the next generation to read and interpret my vision as a composition not a competition!

Happy Reading!

THE THEATRICAL MELODIA OF MY LIFE : CHRONICLE ONE

This book is based on my journey, the roller coaster I call life, my thought patterns, and my experiences. How I overcome so many turmoils, how I changed my perception, for it led me towards a destination that gave me tension. Where I felt I had no freedom or free will; all I had was failure. Added with faith, and the hope to overcome another fall. Feeding off the concept as I rise above it all!

Crucify The Holy Spirit While You Sacrifice A Soul: Chronicle Viii

Crucify the Holy Spirit while you Sacrifice a Soul, Chronicle VIII is the continuation of the Melodia of my life KREA PREA (TM). An Epistemology, My Odyssey call it My Bible I swear by it. The difference is my one speaks in volumes and Chronicles. I speak the truth and in tongue.

It's an original piece, based on my daily life and how I perceive Humanity. Where I had premonitions, and those visions were over powering my thoughts and instincts. Where it may look tedious to some to me it felt poisonous. No time to waste!

The Iconic Door To Peace My Souls Final Feast A True Awakening: Chronicle 22

A technicality to rectify a task from the past arose. It was to bring forth peace, torn at every trace an insightful memory; I was to replace a line up, for a belting. For what the corrupt did, just to speed up the process; was priceless.

Entering The Kingdom Of Oblivion: Chronicle 14

A method that lined me up for a rude awakening. Where the corrupt tracked me down, restored their energy by summoning me. A key, that was stolen from me was relisted and I was returning to retrieve it. I left it to chance, then let my guard down because I was let down.

Majestic Mysticism A Celtic Tradition: Chronicle Xv11

How I survived my daily bread. A journal added by my imagination, and the extension to validate my perception. Where my mission took over my vision and created an opposition.
Whether it is a theory or an indication that I have

a vivid imagination. The world is what it is and I describing the way I see it will help me remember; when where and how I got there. State the facts, create a peace then pause and reflect. All so I can get back on track and resurrect from a tongue wag.

Tetelestai Debt Paid In Full: Chronicle Xx

It is a one woman Comedy Show & I am the Comedian. I am to push forth, and preach my critical analysis. A tell-tale story, to catch up, and catch the corrupt red handed. For their mission, was to belt me to the ground. Just to hide a scam, a scheme a failed proposition in-between. A position to hand me joy, had come around.

A Sinful Act Of Kindness From The Heart : Chronicle 24

Where one day at a time took a wrong turn, a least expected accident turned my life upside down. An unexpected nightmare. Exiting my comfort zone and hit with another dead end.

Burning Crown Of Glory: Chronicle 25

I found myself in a position of questioning the motives of certain individuals. I was put in a situation, that had me forced to override, run hide, and return when needed. The clock was ticking, and those who were relentless and ruthless were scheming. I could not fight back, I felt I was ganged up on.

www.ingramcontent.com/pod-product-compliance
Lightning Source LLC
Chambersburg PA
CBHW020742230426
43665CB00009B/521